BUILDING
CHRISTIAN
FAMILIES

BUILDING

CHRISTIAN

FAMILIES

by
Mitch and Kathy Finley

ThomasMore®
A DIVISION OF TABOR PUBLISHING

Allen, Texas

All quotations from scripture are from the New Revised Standard Version Bible: Catholic Edition, Copyright 1993 and 1989, Division of Christian Education of the National Council of Churches of Christ in the United States of America.

Send all inquiries to:
Thomas More Publishing
200 East Bethany Drive
Allen, Texas 75002–3804

Printed in the United States of America

ISBN 0–88347–335–6

1 2 3 4 5   00 99 98 97 96

CONTENTS

DEDICATION

For the
National Association of Catholic Family Life Ministers

"Truly I tell you, just as you did it to one of the least of these who are members of my family, you did it to me."

Matthew 25:40

Preface to the New Edition

$\mathcal{M}$ore than ten years have passed since the publication of the first edition of this book, entitled *Christian Families in the Real World: Reflections on a Spirituality for the Domestic Church* (Thomas More, 1984). A new and simpler title reflects the purpose of this new edition as a basic guide and inspiration for families of all shapes and sizes.

In 1984, we had been married for ten years, and we were the parents of three young boys, two of them not yet in school. As this new edition goes to press, we have been married for twenty-one years, and our sons are all teenagers in high school. To coin a phrase, time flies. Our convictions about the nature and purpose of a family spirituality remain essentially the same, however. Were we to write the first edition of this book today we might have more to say about the challenge of raising teenagers, but other than that the book would be the same one we wrote more than a decade ago.

Revising our original book involved many stylistic changes and some additions to the text. Here and there we had to cut dated material. The chapter on single-parent and couple-parent families received the most extensive reworking. The original chapter was on single-parent families only, and we wanted to adapt its contents to include the experiences and issues that apply to both single-parent and two-parent families. The two kinds of family are similar in more ways than they are different.

Finally, we dedicate *Building Christian Families* to the Catholic organization that has done more than any other to further the cause of family ministry and the enrichment of family life in the Catholic Church in the United States: The National Association of Catholic Family Life Ministers. We are proud of this organization and proud to have been actively associated with it during its earliest years.

Acknowledgements

In the Foreword to his contemporary classic *The Affluent Society*, economist John Kenneth Galbraith wrote: "Authorship of any sort is a fantastic indulgence of the ego. It is well, no doubt, to reflect on how much one owes to others."

We would like to express our thanks to the following people: Kay Babcock, for valuable insights into the experience of single parents; Clay Barbeau, for inspiration and encouragement; Rev. Donald Conroy, for sharing his enthusiasm for and vision of family ministry and for his support, encouragement, and friendship; Dolores DuPont and her late husband, Bob, for their many years of marriage, their beautiful family, and for welcoming us at their table; Rev. Andrew M. Greeley, for the sociological research he and his colleagues have done on Catholic families today; the couples who serve in the Marriage Preparation Weekends program of the Diocese of Spokane, Washington, for sharing with us their marriages, families, and friendship and for their dedicated example of service to others; Bob and Karen Kopesky, for taking us in when we were "strangers in a strange land" and for showing us what hospitality means; Dan Morris, for inviting us, years ago, to write a weekly column for our diocesan newspaper, thus affording us opportunities to reflect on many of the themes that appear in this book; Rev. Tom Royce, S. J., for sharing himself so readily with families; David M. Thomas, for some of the key theological insights upon which our reflections are based; the community of St. Benedict the Moor Parish, Milwaukee, Wisconsin, for showing us during the mid-1970s what a parish can be; and special thanks to all the families who have helped us to reflect honestly on what building Christian families means.

THE FAMILY IS CHURCH

Introduction

$\mathcal{V}$irtually every major theologian whose subject is the theology of the church has neglected an important insight in the teachings of the Second Vatican Council. There is little evidence in their writings that according to Vatican II the family is the "domestic church." Theologians either ignore this insight or mention it only in passing and show a limited understanding of its implications for both families and the church as a whole.

As Archbishop J. Francis Stafford of the Archdiocese of Denver, Colorado, once observed:

> Since the Council of Trent [1545-63] the church has lost a family dimension in its understanding of religious life . . . We have now relegated most of our religious life to the parish, to the detriment of the families.

Archbishop Stafford continued:

> Very few persons who are studying theology

professionally today give any attention to the religious mysteries of marriage and family life.

Those who belong to families intuitively realize that their faith makes little sense apart from what goes on in the daily experience of family relationships. Together with those who work closely with families, they know that the family—in its various forms—is "the foundational church."

Within the family, the foundational experiences of the Christian life happen best, for both children and adults. For most people, it is within the fabric of family life that faith becomes real. In family life, we experience our deepest joys and our deepest anguish, which means that in family life we most often discover the Cross and Resurrection of Christ in our own experience.

When Vatican II called the family "the domestic church," this was nothing original. The conviction that the family is the most basic religious community predates the church. In Jewish tradition, the home, not the synagogue, is the center of religious life. Some words of Jesus echo the basic New Testament understanding of the church: "Where two or three are gathered in my name, I am there among them" (Matthew 18:20). Whatever else these words may describe, they clearly apply to the Christian family.

When the earliest Christians were banned from the synagogue, they naturally gravitated to private homes. By the late fourth century, St. John Chrysostom—in his sermons on the Book of Genesis and in his commentary on the Epistle to the Ephesians—described the family as *ekklesia,* the Greek Second Testament term for church. Only once did John Chrysostom use the diminutive form *ekklesiola,* "little church"; more often he simply called the family *ekklesia*—church.

In the late nineteenth century, Pope Leo XIII wrote that "the family was ordained of God . . . It was before the church, or rather the first form of the church on earth."

It is particularly significant that the Second Vatican Council discussed the family not in a separate document but in the context of its documents on the church. It's as if the council said that if we are going to talk about the church we must talk about family life too. Also, we can't talk about family life without talking about the church.

In the years following the council, Pope Paul VI frequently recalled that the family is the domestic church. He said that the family is the most basic cell not only of society, but of the church as well. In *Evangelii nuntiandi,* his apostolic exhortation on evangelization, Paul VI spelled out an important implication of this theological insight: "There should be found in every Christian family the various aspects of the entire church."

The Christian family *is* the church in miniature. In the course of his homily at the Mass which opened the 1980 Synod of Bishops, Pope John Paul II gave this insight his own concise formulation when he said that the family is meant to "constitute the church in its fundamental dimension."

While on a visit to the United States in 1987, John Paul II declared again that "the family in fact is the basic unit of society and of the church. It is 'the domestic church.'"

Finally, theologian Bernard Cooke wrote in his 1983 book, *Sacraments and Sacramentality :*

> The Christian family is meant to be the most basic instance of Christian community, people

bonded together by their shared relationship to
the risen Jesus.

All this means that in great part both the local parish
and the universal church depend upon families for their
fundamental vitality as they strive to make Christ present
in the modern world. It also means that as families go, so
goes the church. If we want a strong church in the future,
we must pay attention to family life in the church today. If
we want vocations to the priesthood and religious life,
where do we think these come from most often? From
families, of course—yet another reason to nourish and
support family life in our parishes.

Virtually everyone belongs to a family, a domestic or
home church, in some way. We would, however, limit our
definition of *family* to that articulated by the U. S.
Catholic Conference's Ad Hoc Committee on Marriage
and Family Life. In its 1987 document *A Family Perspective
in Church and Society: A Manual For All Pastoral Leaders*,
the committee defines the family as "an intimate
community of persons bound together by blood, marriage,
or adoption, for the whole of life."

Newly wed couples are a family. Single parent
families are also a true form of home church. Older
couples whose children have grown and childless
couples constitute authentic forms of familial and
ecclesial life.

Priests and vowed religious continue to participate in
their extended family of origin. Relationships with other
priests or religious—whether in a rectory or a religious
community house—can't be called family life, per se. But
religious community life should constitute for priests and
religious at least an echo of family life. Indeed, many

founders of religious orders spoke of the need to model community life after family life.

Single and widowed people of any age still belong to their family of origin and their extended family. Almost always they have a network of primary relationships which serves as a continuing experience of community life. Single people have "family issues" to deal with like everyone else.

Christian tradition and official church teachings clearly maintain that the family, in its various forms, is an authentic and indispensable form of church. Yet the notion that the family is the most basic cell of church life has little impact on the life of the average Catholic. It has little effect on many parishes. Countless homilies and lectures have been delivered since Vatican II on the church as the People of God and Body of Christ. Now and then a diocese latches onto the idea of calling the church a "family" at fund-raising time. But only recently have there been efforts to take seriously the ancient insight that the family is *ekklesia,* the most basic form of church life.

It is time to embrace the truth that the parish depends for its existence on Christian families and that parish and family are interdependent. In the words of a 1979 statement by the Papal Commission for the Family: "This is the time to present the family as the center of the pastoral reflection of the church."

The first form of the church into which an infant is baptized is the church of the family. As pastoral theologians remind us today, the baptism of a baby makes little sense apart from daily opportunities for the growing child to experience the Christian life in his or her family relationships.

Within the family and around the family table, children experience the meaning of the Eucharist long before they receive their First Communion. Within the fabric of life in the domestic church, child and adult experience the meaning of forgiveness and reconciliation, apart from any official sacramental celebration of this experience. In the family, both adults and children experience the Christian life at its most immediate, where the seeds of faith are planted and cultivated daily.

This book is about a spirituality for families, a spirituality suggested by the traditional teaching that the family is *ekklesia*. In particular, this spirituality takes its cues from the words of Paul VI: "There should be found in every Christian family the various aspects of the entire church."

But *spirituality* is one of those timeworn terms that suggests more, and less, than it should. It summons up a split between body and soul, between spirit and flesh, between religious and secular life. We take for granted another understanding of *spirituality*. For the spiritual life takes human nature as a cohesive whole and relates it to the Divine Mystery. A spirituality for families refers as much to family conflict as it does to family prayer. It has as much to do with the day in, day out, relationships between family members as it does with the relationship of faith between the family and God.

Family spirituality means no more and no less than this: A family's ongoing attempts to live every dimension of its life in communion with the Cross and Resurrection of Jesus the Christ. Yet every family is unique in its spirituality as every family has a personality of its own. The Smith family will have a Smith spirituality, the O'Briens an O'Brien spirituality, and the Sanchez family will have a Sanchez spirituality. Of course, each of these unique family spiritualities will also share a common spirit through a shared faith in the presence of Christ who dwells in each family's midst.

This book is based on the conviction that if a family is—in reality and not merely by way of a pious analogy—a genuine form of church, of ecclesial life, then certain principles for a family spirituality and family lifestyle follow quite naturally

If a family is *ekklesia*, then it is first of all to be a community, an intimate network of personal relationships. As a Christian community, the family is also to be of service to one another and to those outside the family who have special needs. The family is to be a community that prays and ritualizes its faith in ways natural to families. Because the spirit and life of the family are guided by the gospel, the family finds itself inclined to adopt attitudes and values which are sometimes countercultural.

The ways God speaks in the scriptures, in the church, and in the events of our times lead families to a new understanding and awareness of the impact of human sexuality on families and on the family roles of men and women. Single-parent and couple-parent families confront unique challenges to be guided and sustained by the Spirit. The home church, in its various forms, is called to proclaim the gospel, to be a light on a hilltop, and the salt of the earth.

The most basic form of family life is marriage. Therefore, a married couple constitutes the smallest possible expression of ecclesial life too. In the traditional two-parent nuclear family, the married couple is the foundation of the foundational church. Parents, through their special role in families, function in a pastoral as well as a socializing capacity.

Finally, the relationship between the domestic church and the parish is an extremely important one. Each form of ecclesial life depends upon and supports the other. In the words of Pope John Paul II:

> Each parish must be fully committed to [the pastoral care of families], especially in the face of so much breakdown and undermining of family life in society.

The following pages present discussions of these topics in the light of their connections to a family spirituality. We intend these reflections to be a stimulus for unique families to discover their own unique spiritualities, not so much a guidebook to consult for specific instructions.

THE FAMILY IS A COMMUNITY

Chapter One

$\mathcal{I}$t is impossible to be Christian apart from a community of faith. It is a contradiction to think of being Christian in isolation from others. Even those rare individuals who receive a special religious calling to live as hermits belong to a human and church community. We all belong, in traditional terms, to "the mystical body of Christ."

This is why we understand the sacrament of baptism today most basically as a sacrament of initiation into the faith community. For to be joined to Christ through baptism is also to be joined to his body, the People of God. The two cannot be separated.

To say that any Christian family is an authentic church community is to say that the first form of Christian community to which a person belongs is his or her family. In terms borrowed from the New Testament tradition, my "neighbor" is first those with whom I live most closely, the other members of my family. These are the neighbors Christ commands us to love.

Families are also hotbeds of conflict. It is at times of family conflict that the "enemy" whom Jesus teaches me to love is also a member of my family. The enemy is that two-year-old who is driving me to delirium, the teenager whose rebellious behavior is carrying me to the brink of an ulcer, or my spouse who continues to squeeze the toothpaste in the middle of the tube, even after all these years.

As a member of a home church, I respond to my Christian vocation by a dedication to building community within my family. This is true regardless of my family's particular configuration—two-parent, single-parent, blended, or a couple without children or whose children are grown and gone.

If my family is the place where I participate in the most fundamental ways in Christian community life, then it is vital for the family as a whole to make a firm commitment to love one another—to actively stay in touch with one another and care for one another. Although the shape this takes will vary (depending on circumstances, such as the ages of children) the need to stay in touch with one another remains constant. This means that as a family, we care enough to be there for one another for no other reason than the fact that we are a family.

The church of the home is a community of baptized Christians. Part of membership in this church community is the willingness—indeed, the enthusiasm—to make time for each other regularly.

In his lectures, author and family counselor Clayton C. Barbeau makes the point that time is not found. (I do not discover ten minutes lying on the sidewalk one day, much as I might come upon a dime someone has dropped by accident.) Rather, time is made. (I make the time to spend on those activities and interests that are of greatest value to me.) I have only a certain amount of time in my day, in my week—in my life. I must take responsibility for deciding how I will use my time.

This is precisely what Christian families must do if they are to build up their relationships with one another and thus build up the Body of Christ in their midst. We must set priorities, with time given to family relationships high on the list. The church of the home has no choice in today's hectic world but to sacrifice some less important interests and activities outside the family circle in order to allow for regular time together. No one can do everything.

The calendar of a typical Christian family is filled with commitments to many activities and organizations which, rather than bringing the family together, fragment it further. Most of these involvements are with "good" and "worthy" causes: parish social activities, day-care co-ops, parish educational programs, school-related sports programs, civic organizations that depend on volunteer help, Scouting programs. . . . The list is endless.

A renewed awareness of the importance of nourishing family relationships demands that the Christian family make sacrifices as an expression of love. No one—and no family—can participate in all the worthwhile or attractive opportunities for involvement outside the family that naturally come along. When I decide to do this, I cannot do that.

If staying in touch with one another and staying close to one another's lives is the high value that it must be for the Christian family today, then something on the calendar will have to go—for all the members of the family. Involvement in one sport at school instead of two; joining the school newspaper staff and skipping the spring drama production; helping out with the Cub Scouts, but saying "sorry" to the parish fund drive. Perhaps there will be a need for the whole family to live with the sacrifices necessary because Dad or Mom must say no to a promotion that would bring in more money, but would also require that parent to spend more time away from the family.

Here is the operative principle: If an outside activity will increase stress on the family for a significant length of time, the answer should be no. If it will help the family's life to be less stressful, the answer should be yes.

Of course, once the family decides to make time to be together regularly, there are many ways to spend this time. Some families designate one night a week as family night. Not a few families get into the family night habit by trying it for a month or six weeks—perhaps during Lent—to see how it goes. All agree to keep this night free from other involvements. Everyone stays home or we all go together to some shared activity outside the home. Even when kids are teenagers who feel compelled to distance themselves from their family, there can be times for family togetherness.

This can be a time for simple forms of shared prayer, time to talk about how each person's life is going, time for some laughter, time to simply enjoy one another. The point is that the family decides on some mutually agreeable way to be together regularly, to overcome the fragmentation that tends to afflict families today. This is the time to make some effort toward keeping family relationships intimate instead of allowing them to become superficial.

Family times together are times for preventive maintenance. We spend an hour or two preventing generation gaps. We do what we can to prevent our house from becoming little more than a refueling station and a place to sleep. We take positive steps to love one another in ways that can be felt.

An appointment calendar distributed by the advertising department of a newspaper has little blurbs scattered throughout its pages, motivational messages from the newspaper offering the savvy of the marketplace to prospective purchasers of advertising space. One bit of commercial wisdom states: "You can get more buying action when you get your advertising message into the family circle."

How does that "bit of wisdom" make you feel? From the perspective of the American marketplace, the family is first of all a gathering of consumers, and some of the "market value" of the family arises precisely from the individual's membership in a family. Families are where most babies live, and babies are a multi-billion-dollar-a-year business. Parents spend billions of dollars a year on weddings. Parents feel pressure to keep their offspring dressed in a stylish fashion.

Because the average North American family is typically isolated from other families—usually in every way but geographically—each family must have its own washing machine, lawnmower, ladder, television set, and car. So a family is primarily a market, a buyer of consumer goods.

The living room of the American family has become, through the presence of television, the primary target for advertising campaigns. The Christian family must recover its role as the primary molder of the spirit of its members. We are not primarily consumers. Rather, we are persons who need one another more than we need more possessions. In a world of strangers, the members of a family must take the trouble to remain close to one another. This decision will bring a family into conflict with a materialistic value system which proclaims that human happiness and fulfillment are found through the buying and accumulation of more and more possessions.

Families will encounter other obstacles in their effort to nourish healthy family relationships. Consider the secular value of privacy. In our world today, privacy is all but an ultimate value. The more bathrooms in a family's home, the better. Most American homes have two or more television sets. That way, if a parent doesn't like what the kids are watching, she or he can avoid conflict by moving to another room and another television set. Not only do we not communicate with one another while watching TV, we also watch different programs in different rooms.

The point is not that multiplying bathrooms or television sets destroys family life by itself. Rather, when such facts tend to characterize our family living arrangements, we need to be sensitive to their possible negative impact on family relationships and take countermeasures to prevent or mitigate the negative effects.

Another ideal of the American family is for each family member who is old enough to drive to have his or her own car. That way, no one need take anyone else into account when making plans that require the use of a car. Again, the goal is to prevent conflict.

If the behavior of many families is any gauge, it would seem that each member of the family has a right to eat what he or she wants, when he or she wants it. The idea of three family meals at regular times each day is archaic! The family meal, at least in the evening, is the last holdout for many families as a time to be together once a day.

But even the evening meal as a family time is a rarity for many families. The family meal is an endangered species. "After all," goes the refrain, "how can parents expect everyone to be present at the same time for dinner?" Daughter has tennis practice and Son is on the baseball team! And besides, Dad is working overtime this month. Often the schedules are in charge of the family, instead of vice versa.

Many families that share an evening meal do so with the television set turned on, usually tuned to a news program. Together we stare at the Tube, together we stuff food in our mouths. Probably our together time is punctuated by one-liners hurled at the program being watched and at one another. Throughout the entire process—before we stampede in our different directions for the evening—rarely do human forms of interaction take place that could not occur between strangers.

I crave human intimacy. But I want my privacy. Intimacy means, among other things, conflict. I don't like conflict; it's too painful. I don't want to deal with the difficulties I will encounter if I make an effort to be with the other members of my family. (Oh, the anguish of only one bathroom.) Community means to share, cooperate, compromise, and let others go first. It's far easier to run for my private room or jump into my private car and drive to my terribly important meeting. It's much easier to escape my longing for intimacy by joining another crowd of people with whom I do not have to be intimate or by turning on a television set.

That's the crux of the matter: Intimacy requires the willingness to live with interpersonal conflict, the commitment to work through differences and problems to stay close to one another.

The ideal for the family-church of the home is the readiness to accept the painful times for the sake of continued closeness and a living family community. There is one aspect of an authentic family spirituality here: I accept the cross of conflict because I know that it is necessary if we are to experience the resurrection joy of family unity. In the long run, it's the only way.

Another positive step some families take is to schedule a regular family meeting. This is time set aside not so much for nourishing family relationships directly, although in its own way the family meeting definitely contributes to this. Rather, it is time to work. We deal with practical issues and resolve conflicts. The family meeting is a time to air difficulties, voice gripes, make decisions, assign household tasks. A family meeting is the ideal time to decide where we will go for our vacation or to choose the shared Lenten or Christmas activities we will have this year.

At the family meeting, parents can share with youngsters some of the important decisions that will have an impact on the entire family. What about this new job Dad has been offered that would mean moving halfway across the country? Mom thinks she would like to quit her part-time job and return to school. What do the kids think about her not being there when they come home in the afternoon? The more parents share such issues and decisions with their offspring, the more included, trusted, and valued kids will feel.

All kinds of practical issues are dealt with in a family meeting. One family tells the story of their four-year-old son who brought up objections to the requirement that he take a daily nap. Another family—a single-parent family—swears that their relationships with one another depend on the regular family meeting. This gives them a time to face and deal creatively with the often unique issues of a single-parent family. The single parent in this family, a mother, refers to this regular family meeting as "our lifeline to one another."

Placing the emphasis today on the need for family togetherness times is surely appropriate. If the family/church of the home is to be any kind of Christian community at all, there must be regular quality time together. But remember: each family member is also an individual. Words from Thomas Merton, the great Trappist monk and hermit, in *Contemplation in a World of Action* come to mind:

> Are our efforts to be more "communal" and to be more "family" really genuine, or are they only new ways to be intolerant of the solitude and integrity of the individual person?

It is also important for families to value time for the individual to be alone. But privacy is not the theme here. Privacy tends to be little more than a socially acceptable way to talk about avoiding other people. We have already seen that such privacy can have destructive effects on a family. Rather, the alone time that is important for the Christian family is best described as solitude.

In times of quiet solitude, the individual can form some of his or her deepest convictions about life and about his or her relationships with other members of the family. One of the paradoxes of solitude is that when I experience time in this "holy aloneness" my relationships with others are nourished in special ways. I do not seek solitude as an escape from life or from my family. On the contrary, I enter into solitude in order to renew my relationship with the God who is Love and remains at the very heart of my relationships with the other members of my family.

Families that strive to become Christian communities will encourage their members to love this kind of solitude. Parents can best model a love for solitude—for time alone with oneself and God—for children of all ages by talking about their own need for solitary time and how good it is for them. Then, most importantly, they can follow through on their words by making regular time for solitary thought, meditative reading, and quiet prayer. I cannot give what I do not have. I cannot give some peace, a bit of wisdom, and a spirit of joy to my family unless I first gain these for myself.

Some families schedule a day or a weekend every month or two for each parent—and each child who is old enough and so inclined—to be away at a local retreat house, house of prayer, or some other valued place of solitude.

Places such as houses of prayer must be sensitive to the unique scheduling needs of family members who can rarely set aside large blocks of time for retreats and yet need to have time for prayerful solitude—even if there is a thirty-day retreat for priests or sisters going on. It is frustrating for family people to call a house of prayer and be told that they cannot spend a day there because the place is packed with women religious making a thirty-day retreat. Thirty days! This is an unheard of luxury falling on the ears of a parent. Could not one room be kept unoccupied by a house of prayer, even during the heavy summer retreat months, for family people whose spiritual needs continue to exist?

Family members then talk—as part of a family night, around the dinner table, or at some other natural time—about their solitary times, about what they have learned or gained. This tends to inspire a healthy curiosity in kids about spending time in solitude, too, as they become older.

There is perhaps no greater gift parents can offer their children than the gift of a love for regular quiet time alone—time to think, to get to know oneself and God. In today's society, where "the crowd" tends to dominate the individual—especially during the teen years—such youngsters are more likely to grow up with an ability to think for themselves and act as mature Christians, rather than wander through life going along in order to get along.

There is a need for families to be together; a need for children and parents to stay in touch, to talk, to share their lives, their hopes and dreams, their memories, their fears and anxieties. In order for such times to happen, family members may need to make sacrifices on a regular basis. But there is a need, also, for individual family members to become strong in themselves, in what they believe and in their relationship with Christ. For this, regular times of prayerful solitude are vitally importance. By being solitary in fruitful ways and by being together in ways that nourish family intimacy, the Christian family can become an authentic Christian community of faith, hope, and love.

It is this life as a Christian family community that forms the basis for all that remains to be said here about a lifestyle and spirituality for Christian families, those who constitute the church of the home.

THE FAMILY AS SERVANT CHURCH

Chapter Two

$\mathcal{S}$cripture scholars tell us that the core of the message of Jesus appears in Mark 1:15. There Jesus begins his public ministry with these words: "The time is fulfilled, and the kingdom of God has come near; repent, and believe in the good news."

This message has two parts. One part communicates comfort. The other should unsettle us and send us forth on the Christian trek. First, Jesus says that "the kingdom of God has come near." These are words of comfort; words that tell us of the eruption of God's love in human history in a unique manner, as well as in our personal lives. There is no need for fear or anxiety, because just behind life and the universe, indeed bursting into our ordinary days when it is least expected, is the boundless love of God.

But then the other shoe falls. Jesus says, "repent, and believe in the good news." The good news, of course, is the news of God's love for us. We are invited to turn away from self-centered pursuits, from dependence on false gods, in order to believe in and depend on that love alone. This is the only way we can know God. We are called to empty our hearts of fear and distrust, to turn loose of false gods with their false promises, and to embrace the true God and one another in authentic caring love.

In other words, Christ invites the church—and in a special way, the church that is the family—to live a life centered on God and neighbor. The neighbors we are called to love first, of course, are the other members of our family. But it can't stop there. There is a danger that a family may turn in on itself. We may begin to feel so cozy and warm in our family relationships that we forget the call to reach out to others. Just as the church at large is sent to minister to those outside the community who have special needs, so the family-church is sent by Christ to touch the lives of those in the wider community with the love and peace with which they themselves are blessed by God.

To reach out to those who do not belong to our immediate family is an essential part of a family spirituality. There is no better illustration of how important this is than the story of the sheep and the goats told by Jesus in Matthew 25. This is the only place in the New Testament where we hear, in explicit terms, what will determine our eternal destiny.

The message in Matthew is not that one must believe certain doctrines or go to church on Sunday. These things are important, of course, but only in a secondary or derivative way. The critical question is "How do we meet the needs of those who thirst and hunger, those who are need clothing and those in jail?" What matters in the end is to meet basic human needs with compassionate action. This is the mark of a faith that is more than words and pious genuflections.

The family-church is invited by the Christ who dwells in the family's midst to turn outward to others, to overcome the temptation to turn in on itself. So the Christian family will naturally feel inspired to discover how they can best put their gifts at the service of others. Whatever decision we make about this, one principle is especially important to keep in mind: Whatever the family decides to do to serve others, it must be some form of service that the whole family can become involved in together. Serving others should not become another way to fragment the family! This would be self-defeating.

In *Bleak House*, Charles Dickens paints a brilliant literary portrait of the classic do-gooder whose many works of "charity" constantly cause her own family to suffer. Mrs. Jellyby is forever dashing away to save the natives in "Borioboolagah, on the banks of the Niger," while at home her own children are dirty and ill cared for and her husband is sullen and withdrawn. This is an extreme example, of course, but Mrs. Jellyby's situation illustrates what can happen if parents become so involved in helping others that they spend less and less time with their own children. This is an excellent way to sow resentment in the hearts of children which could easily be transferred, perhaps unconsciously, to Christianity and the church as a whole.

Instead, when the family regularly serves together this has positive impact on both parents and children. Indeed, involvement in outreach activities alongside their parents is one of the best forms of religious education any youngster can receive. This way children learn from experience that faith is a way of life, that a Christian commitment makes a real difference in the ways one chooses to use the time of one's life. Keep in mind, of course, that no child— especially in adolescence—should be forced to participate in such activities against his or her will.

Service activities generously pursued make it almost impossible for a charge of hypocrisy to be leveled at parents—a charge teenage offspring have on more than one occasion been know to level against parents who appear to be little more than "Sunday Christians."

The Christian family is not, of course, required to become a miniature St. Vincent De Paul Society. Rare families do choose to orient their entire life toward serving others by becoming as a family, for example, members of a Catholic Worker House of Hospitality. Now and then whole families will join Maryknoll or another overseas missionary society for a few years. But for most families the need to serve others is integrated into ordinary day-to-day life.

The ways families choose to do this are as varied as families themselves. But perhaps the most basic spirit that characterizes this aspect of a family spirituality is one of hospitality—a spirited openness to others from outside the family circle. This spirit of hospitality finds its roots in the practice of the earliest Christian families who set aside a "Christ room" in their homes for the wandering pilgrim. This is a tradition largely lost sight of. Even so, many modern families would find it a luxury indeed to be able to let a whole bedroom sit empty most of the time.

But the authentic spirit of hospitality is another matter. This is a spirit that receives the visitor or guest with open arms. Parents set the tone for the family in this regard. Any parish includes families who are forever inviting others over to dinner on Sunday afternoons. Many a parish has its unofficial "welcome family." This family has an abundance of warmth, humor, and cheerful conversation but is not interested in impressing anyone with its house, which is usually filled with furniture that stopped trying to look new long ago and with kitchen walls covered with the scrawled drawings of children. Invited to the home of such a family, we can count on not being treated like a guest. Instead, we find ourselves helping to put together the lasagna or toss the salad. Or we may be put to work setting the table, after having been "forced" to accept a refreshing beverage or snack.

Every shape of chair in the house may be drummed into service as family and guests gather around the table. Table prayer is likely to be more boisterous than reverent, and gasps of mock horror are likely to greet the guests' offer to help clear the table and wash the dishes.

Some families have a special gift for taking in foster or adoptive children. Such families often tell stories of how this form of service changed and enriched their lives and the lives of their long-term guests. Often the parents' own birth children consider themselves to be as involved and important to the success of these efforts as are the adults. This form of service is special indeed, in that it brings the most intimate fabric of the family's life to bear on the lives of youngsters who have known precious little love in their few years.

Another form of service that is becoming more common is that of providing a temporary home for girls or young women who are pregnant and unmarried, during the time when they are awaiting the birth of their babies. In a time when so much is heard about the abortion issue, this is a concrete way in which those who claim to be pro-life can put flesh on their words. Pointing an accusing finger at those who undergo abortions is easy. Offering an alternative in the form of time, money, concern, and the need for a whole family to adapt lovingly for several months to the presence of a new member (one struggling with a crisis situation) is another thing!

Groups of married couples often help engaged couples prepare for marriage. One group of couples decided they wanted to be involved in such a program, but they did not want to leave their children in the care of others to do this. So they designed a program independent of any national-level organization, a program which allows them to bring their children along. Indeed, they designed the program so the children would not only be there, but would contribute in a positive way to the quality of the experience offered the engaged couples.

The program is organized in a weekend format and held at a retreat center, as many are. But children are expected to be there and to be in evidence. During registration times, recreation, and meals, the engaged couples naturally interact with the children. During times when the married couples work with the engaged couples in formal ways, the teenagers and older children care for the younger ones. Thus the overall atmosphere established is one not just of marriage, but of family.

It is typical for engaged couples who attend this program to comment positively on the contribution made by the children to their learning experience. They remark on how much more realistic it is to attend a marriage preparation program with children around than to have a more sterile, adults-only experience—as if children would not someday be an important part of marriage for them too.

In another part of the country, families for miles around participate in a hot meal program sponsored by an inner-city parish. Teams are organized so that a different team prepares, brings in, and serves a hot meal each evening of the month, six nights a week. On most teams, there are families with children of all ages. It is moving for the newcomer to witness moms, dads, and kids all serving up the simple but nutritious food on a bitterly cold winter evening to street people, homeless families, poor people, people kicked around by the world for years.

Together, the families then sit down to share the food. Everyone gives; everyone receives. Little children chat and giggle with grizzled, unattractive men who a few minutes before were swearing and cursing the fates out on a street corner. Working women and mothers tell bag ladies about the recipe for that evening's hash or dessert. Even the emotionally or mentally ill guests who choose to keep to themselves in some corner of the hall seem to benefit from the spirit brought to this gathering by families.

On the meal ticket each person receives before entering to eat are these words: "Welcome to the Lord's Banquet, the Miracle of Loaves and Fishes." Although the distinctions blur considerably between those who are "doing" and those who are being "done unto," this is another way in which families, as families, reach out to others. Not only do they help those who have less, but they keep before their mind's eye the easily forgotten truth that the world is bigger than just their family with its small agonies and ecstasies.

One family inherited a small lake cabin, not a particularly fancy one, but one that "serves." Since they can usually inhabit the cabin only on weekends, they invite friends and relatives, the parish priest, and the people next door to use it whenever they are free to do so. This family believes they were given their cabin not for themselves alone but to share with others too.

Another family spent several summer weekends helping an elderly neighbor fix up her house, which had sadly deteriorated since her husband's death. They did yard work; painted; cleaned; and repaired screens, storm windows, and plumbing. This family is typical of families who are sensitive to the needs of others as they arise and not so tied up by their own plans and schedules that they cannot respond spontaneously and without fanfare to the ordinary needs of a neighbor.

A young husband and wife with no children of their own yet hop in their car to spend most of one Saturday a month driving around to the homes of others collecting reusable baby supplies for redistribution by a pregnancy care agency. Thus they resist the unique kind of narcissism which can easily afflict the lives of young childless couples in our society today.

One of the activities Jesus mentions in the Matthew 25 story of the sheep and goats is visiting those in prison. What would the impact be if families from parishes located near prisons were to develop ways to serve prisoners and their families? A very simple way for a family to touch the life of a prison inmate is to correspond with him or her by mail. Such a commitment may lead to a personal visit at the prison later on, but whether this happens or not, both the life of the prisoner and the life of the family will be affected in ways consistent with the gospel.

All this said, the most basic form of service happens within the family itself. We serve one another in many small, unspectacular ways, and these are genuine forms of Christian service. We need to give ourselves more credit for this than we often do.

There are as many ways to serve—both within and outside the family—as there are families. The crucial thing is for family members to know that Christ calls them to engage in what used to be known as "the corporal works of mercy." Christ calls the family to give of its time and resources regularly in order to care for those who have special needs, be they physical, emotional or material. This is where the faith that is ritualized in family prayer and in parish liturgies takes on a credibility recognizable a mile away.

The Family Prays and Celebrates

Chapter Three

*O*rdinarily, when family spirituality is mentioned, the first thing people think of is family prayer and other explicit forms of family piety. It should be clear by now that family prayer is but one part of a total family spirituality. Family prayer and celebration are expressions or manifestations of the family's identity as a Christian community, but they are not the identity itself. What makes the family Christian is a common dedication to Christ and the ongoing shared attempt to live the spirit of the gospel.

The family is not Christian, is not the home church, because the family prays together. Rather, because of the faith of the family, the shared personal relationship with the risen Christ, the family prays and celebrates its faith in various ways. Prayer and celebration are expressions before they are causes of faith. Prayer and family liturgies strengthen and nourish our faith as a family. But they are meaningful only to the extent that they are expressions of a family faith that is already there.

Granted, this sounds like something of a chicken-and-egg business, asking which comes first—faith or prayer.

But the purpose of going into the issue is to establish that a family does not become Christian merely by praying. It does so by dedicating itself to Christ and to love of God and neighbor. Only then do family prayer and liturgy attain their most complete character as a way to nourish and fulfill the identity of the family as a Christian community.

That said, it is true that an indispensable part of a family spirituality is regular shared prayer and family rituals. The most important principle is this: family prayer and family ritual ought never to be imposed or artificial. Instead, family prayer must be allowed to emerge from within the fabric of family life itself. We can't make it happen so much as we can nourish its growth in our midst.

The life of the family is itself holy. It is a mistake to act as if we must make it holy by artificial means. The family is a faith community or is called to be such. All we need do is look at the life of the family to discover the naturally sacred events that already take place there. The family recognizes the sacred character of these events and takes simple steps to celebrate that sacred character through prayer and ritual.

It is critical to begin with the most obvious aspects of family life. Start small and keep it simple. For example, there is no more holy event in the life of a family than the family meal. The family's evening meal is naturally eucharistic. At the evening meal, much more can be shared than food. There are opportunities for some prayer, a bit of song, a lighted candle, a brief holding of hands around the table. By taking some simple steps, the family meal can be rescued from its current position on the endangered species list.

Granted, dinnertime can be filled with noise and conflict, sometimes degenerating into near chaos. People jump up from the table at odd times. The baby is screaming; there are arguments over who got the biggest piece of cake and what so-and-so did or did not say at school that day. All the same, the family's evening meal has the potential to be much more. It can be an explicitly sacred event, too, at least some of the time.

Starting when children are little helps. Build traditions around the family table. When our three children were hardly even talking, we began the tradition of singing the refrain from "O Come, O Come, Emmanuel" as the beginning of our grace before dinner during the Advent season. Before long, the little ones were joining in. Even the crying baby would clam up and gaze in delighted wonder around the table at his singing family. Oh, it took Dad and Mom a few evenings of this before a bit of embarrassment at singing in that situation wore off. But just try to call off the singing once and see what a storm of protest would be raised from the hearts of children.

It wasn't long before our family was singing during the Christmas and Easter seasons too. It got to the point where we sang the refrain from one song or another virtually every evening of the year. When our kids reached adolescence and various degrees of religious skepticism set in, we found ourselves relying on the old Catholic standard "Bless us, O Lord, and these thy gifts."

Evening mealtime needs to be sacred for the Christian family. "Is nothing sacred anymore?" goes the saying. For the Christian family, the evening meal is special. This does not mean that there should not be an exception now and then. But as a general rule, all should be present, even when sacrifices must be made for this to be so. This is the one time of day when we promise to be there for one another. The running will stop, the world will turn loose of us as individuals, and we will be a family for twenty minutes or so.

In the long run, nothing that takes us away from one another is as important as our relationships within the family. Nothing. Therefore, we join hands for prayer around a lighted candle—even if Tommy is only holding Linda's little finger because tonight girls are "yucky." We are family because of the real presence of Christ in our midst. Two or three (or four or five or six. . .) are gathered together in the name of Jesus.

The family meal is time to celebrate special days in simple but meaningful ways, special days both sacred and secular. For since the Son of God has shared our life and our world as one of us, all times and all events are holy; the secular is inseparable from the sacred. Even events in our lives that appear to have no sacred dimension do include the sacred if we but look a little closer.

One of the most obvious secular-sacred events is a birthday. When a family gathers to celebrate the birthday of one of its members around the dinner table, more is marked than the passage of the anniversary of a birth. What is birth? It is creation, the coming into existence of the totally new and unique.

To celebrate a birthday is to wonder anew at the gift of this person to the rest of us. We thank God for Sean, our firstborn. We celebrate Gretchen or Erin or Joseph, Mom or Dad. We light a single candle in the center of the table to remind us of Christ present in our midst. Today, we also light the candles on the cake and sing "Happy Birthday." But we also say a special prayer of thanks for the birthday person, mentioning his or her special qualities or special events in the life of this person since last year's birthday. We pray to acknowledge that birthday gifts remind us of the birthday person who is the most valued gift of all today.

For years we have kept a "Family Book of Days," a three-ring binder of blank pages, pages filled now with reminders of significant dates in the life of our family, in the lives of our extended family and friends, and in the lives of saints and other remarkable people we admire. There is one page for each day of the year.

Open the book to today's date: There is the reminder that today is the feast of St. Clare. How many knew she is the patron saint of television? Turn another page—next week will mark the anniversary of the death of Thomas Merton. Last month we remembered the anniversary of the birth of Dorothy Day, and before long we will be recall the day on which our second son took his first steps. Remember the day Jim fell out of the apple tree and broke his arm? How about the time Aunt Barbara gave birth to twins! Here is the day the Wright Brothers made their first flight at Kitty Hawk—which is also Dad's birthday!

Part of an evening meal ritual might be to open and read the Family Book of Days, just before prayer or during the meal itself. This is one way we build family traditions. Thus do we help preserve our shared memories which give us strength and much joy. It is, in great part, our shared memories that bond us to one another, that make us a family.

In this way, too, we remember that we are part of a much larger family, one that transcends both history and geographical location. Our larger family—traditionally called the communion of saints—spans the centuries and encompasses both heaven and earth. With all of these we are one; we are family.

Many typical events—both special and ordinary—can be observed with prayer and simple rituals around the family table. This is important because in this way a normal, natural event takes on special meaning: The family is not asked to gather on some artificial pretext, and the family's ordinary life is not disrupted by prayer and ritual. Instead, the ordinary family meal is allowed to express the sacred dimensions of the family's life that are always there,

Some of the most unlikely "secular" events lend themselves to sacred celebrations around the family dinner table. Say a teenager receives his or her driver's license. Light the Christ candle on the table in the usual manner. Include in the table prayer a petition for the safety of the young driver (and of the family car!) but include also an acknowledgment of the new level of responsibility and maturity this event signals in the life of the young person. Include a prayer of thanks for the driver's test successfully passed. Pray that the faith of the young person may grow along with this sign of secular maturity. Conclude with a round of applause from the entire family.

How about the first day of school? Or the beginning of a new job or career? The anticipated beginning of a family journey the next morning lends itself beautifully to the use of some of the traditional prayers for going on a journey. The list of events that can be celebrated around the family table goes on and on. Just a little creativity and courage are required.

There are other natural events in the life of the family that lend themselves to ritual and prayer. Going to sleep and waking up are laden with religious meaning. As the pastors of the home church, parents have the privilege of blessing their children. From their youngest years, parents may give their children a blessing at bedtime. The parent simply traces the sign of the cross on the child's forehead—as he or she did at the child's baptism—and says, "God bless you," "Christ's peace be with you," or some other simple prayer. The parent concludes by placing her or his hand lightly on the child's head for a moment. Or any parent can think up a way of doing this that she or he is comfortable with. Children love this blessing and soon would not think of going to bed without it.

Finally, there are the more obvious liturgical seasons of the year which lend themselves to family home celebrations. Advent is time for the Advent calendar. It's surprising how affection for this calendar maintains a hold on children, even when they become "too old" for such things. This is the season, of course, for a family Advent wreath, to be lighted every evening for the family meal in place of the usual single Christ candle.

Then comes Christmas time. Make of the decorating of the home and of the tree a time to remember the often missed sacred nature of Christmas. Put some sacred Christmas music on the record player or stereo. Bless the tree and manger scene as well.

During Lent, substitute a dish of sand or an old dead branch from a tree (small, of course) for the Christ candle on the table. Begin the family grace with the refrain from a favorite Lenten song. Revive an old parish custom and adapt it for the home: Cover all religious art in the home with a purple cloth—the crucifix, an icon on the wall, or a statue. This tangible way to mark the season can have a profound impact on children.

Next, of course, comes Easter. Use an Easter song for the table prayer. Bring back the Christ candle. Bake an Easter bread. Decorate eggs and talk about the egg as a symbol of the Resurrection. Especially when children are old enough, be sure the family goes together to the Easter-eve liturgy. Traveling to church in the darkness of the early spring adds to the drama of the liturgy with its symbols of fire and water, of darkness, light, and exultation. Go to almost any lengths to avoid a dull, lifeless liturgy on Easter!

There are so many good resource books on family prayer and celebration that this chapter is purposely brief and sketchy. Finally, however, this must be said: We learn family prayer and family home liturgies slowly. They cannot, in truth, be taught. Each unique family must adapt and modify any "recipe." Each family must learn by trial and error and success what is good for its family members and what is not.

There are problems to be overcome too. There is the pain of the family where one parent is interested but the other is reluctant. Teens, unless they grew up with family prayer—and sometimes even then—may resist the suggestion that they participate in a family ritual. These are difficult situations, and there are no magic solutions.

In the end, a family prays by praying. We begin by beginning. We can best answer the question "How can we pray as a family?" with encouragement to begin, to be patient with ourselves and with one another, and to be persistent. The family that starts in little ways, that does not expect to become a family that prays with ease at the drop of a saint's feast day, is most likely to succeed by degrees.

The secret of all prayer, including family prayer, is to begin by quietly praying for the gift of prayer. In praying together around our table for the gift of prayer, we begin to pray. Our prayer will have already been answered, and prayer will bloom in our midst, growing and nourishing the spirit of family life—not without purposeful efforts and not without some sacrifice, but nourishing the family's life in hidden ways all the same.

MARRIAGE: FOUNDATION FOR THE HOME CHURCH

Chapter Four

$\mathcal{T}$he foundation for the traditional nuclear family is the relationship of wife and husband. Upon the couple depends the quality of life in the family as a whole. As Jesuit theologian Karl Rahner made clear, the married couple constitutes the smallest authentic form of church:

> In marriage the church is made present. It is really the smallest community, the smallest, but at the same time the true community of the redeemed and the sanctified . . . the smallest, but at the same time the genuine individual church.

Therefore, the sacrament of marriage is best understood as a specific way of being church, of living as a Christian community. It is the vocation of the married couple to be Christians precisely by being married to each other.

Let's be even more precise about this. The most basic of all the sacraments is baptism. Through baptism, the Christian life begins; we inaugurate life in Christ. The sacraments of vocation—holy orders and matrimony—are ways to live one's baptismal commitment, ways to channel one's Christian life along specific lines.

A spirituality of marriage, then, is best understood in those ways in which the couple live out the baptismal commitment in their relationship with each other, first of all, and then in their relationships with their children and with the rest of the world. But we must always keep in mind that uppermost in the spirituality of marriage is the intimacy of husband and wife.

In order to understand a spirituality of marriage, it's important to have a prior understanding of baptism. For only if we understand baptism correctly can we view marriage as a way to live the baptismal promises.

In years past, baptisms were, as a rule, held off in a corner of the parish church in a private manner, when nothing else was going on. About the only time Catholics witnessed a baptism was when their own children were born or when they were asked to be godparents to someone else's child. Even then the baptismal ceremony was wrapped in Latin, so the rite of baptism itself hardly communicated a complete understanding of the sacrament.

Today it is more common for infant and adult baptisms to be celebrated in the context of regularly scheduled parish masses—and, of course, in the vernacular. This reminds the entire congregation several times a year of the promises we make at baptism and of the beliefs we affirm. The words of the baptismal liturgy are more familiar today than they have been for centuries. But what is the meaning of those words?

Perhaps we may understand baptism today by calling on insights from the Fourth Gospel. There the Christian community learns that as disciples of Christ they live in the world and for the world but that the Christian is not "of the world." In other words, Christians are to be closely involved in the concerns of the world but according to a different set of values and standards than those embraced by "the world" insofar as it is unchanged by the Spirit of Christ. This also means that the Christian recognizes and celebrates and takes joy in the world since God created it and Christ redeemed it. The Christian rejects the world only insofar as it is less than God intended it to be.

According to the gospel tradition, therefore, the Christian's priorities are unique. The Christian finds the meaning of life in relationships with God and neighbor. This is why Jesus teaches that the greatest commandment is to love God with one's whole being and one's neighbor as oneself. This is radical talk! For the Christian's life is to be focused entirely on a dedication to love of God and neighbor.

This idea is so central to the Christian perspective that in the only place in any of the Gospels—Matthew 25—that Jesus discusses what will determine one's eternal destiny, he zeros right in on the need to care for one's neighbor. Jesus identifies the love of God with compassionate action on behalf of those with special human needs. He says that if we visited those in prison, clothed the naked, or fed the hungry, we did it for him.

The heart of the Christian life is compassionate love of God and neighbor, and the two cannot be separated. The business of going to church on Sunday and believing certain doctrines constitutes something that is secondary—important, but secondary all the same.

When people remarked on the lives of the first Christians, they did not say, "Those Christians, see how they go to church and believe certain doctrines!" Sounds ludicrous, doesn't it? No, as everyone knows, the comment was "See those Christians, how they love one another!"

This is what makes the Christian way of life unique; this is what being a follower of Christ is most basically about: a dedication to loving action on behalf of God and other people as the most fundamental standard upon which one's daily life is based. It's as simple, as radical—and as difficult—as that.

If we are to understand marriage correctly, then, and if we are to make a Christian spirituality of marriage explicit, we must do so in light of this understanding of the Christian life. The Christian life is a matter of living in the world and on behalf of the world and its concerns but according to a set of values and attitudes which place love of God and neighbor at the heart of one's life. This is what Christian marriage is about: going about the business of living in and for the world—of loving the world—by placing love of God and other people uppermost.

But we need to make this understanding still more precise. The point here is that married couples constitute the smallest form of church because they dedicate themselves to love of God and neighbor as married people. Every expression they may give to their faith is conditioned by this fact. In every sense, the married partners are followers of Christ in the world by being married to one another. To paraphrase St. Paul, they may give all they have to feed the poor and hand over their bodies to be burned, but if they do not have a loving and lively marriage it profits them nothing.

This gets to the heart of the matter. For Christian spouses, the neighbor they are to love is first of all the person to whom they are married. To nourish and give regular attention to the marriage relationship is central to the couple's living of the Christian life. The couple's faith life is not something apart from their daily life together; rather, it remains at the heart of their marital experience.

To paraphrase from the New Testament again (1 John): If anyone says, "My love is fixed on God," but fails to love his or her spouse, that person is a liar. One who shows no active love for the spouse he or she can see every morning across the breakfast table cannot love the God he or she cannot see. The commandment we have from God is this: Whoever loves God must also love his or her spouse in ways that can be felt.

This may sound dreamy and idealistic, like a lot of nice words that almost anyone would agree with—and then promptly forget. Perhaps the question to ask at this point is "So what?"

Here we have a set of ideas which, if correctly understood, lead to a perspective on life that runs directly counter to a view of marriage that dominates the lives of many married couples today. For the Christian married couple there is nothing more important than the ongoing love and intimacy shared by wife and husband.

A contrary perspective holds the upper hand today. The prevailing assumption is that a happy marriage depends upon all kinds of material and economic realities, realities which take first place in the life of the couple. A consumer culture encourages this attitude toward marriage from the moment the engagement is first announced.

The message broadcast to engaged couples is that the future success of their marriage depends on how much money they spend on the engagement ring. Then their future happiness depends on how elaborate the wedding and reception can be. Next, the more money the couple spend on their honeymoon, the more likely that their marriage will be a good one. And we're off and running: our marriage will be all it can be only if we have a big beautiful house filled with new furniture and appliances—even if we must go deeply into debt for this to be possible. And of course. we really do need a brand new car before we can feel really married.

This may sound ridiculous. But it is important to realize that, even if a married couple would not agree with such messages as stated here, everyone is affected by the commercialization of marriage. An almost inescapable mass-media advertising industry presents such messages about marriage in hundreds of ways every day.

Those who manufacture products and offer services to consumers don't pay millions of dollars a year for those thirty- and sixty-second ads on television because they like to spend the money. They do it because it works. And the same can be said for all forms of advertising. They work. Mass-media advertising affects everyone, even though in many cases people are unaware that they are being influenced. The advertising industry very effectively shapes personal values of a superficial and materialistic nature.

Of course, once the couple is married the same set of superficial materialistic values begin to take other forms. We won't be truly good parents unless we buy all kinds of special furniture, clothes, and gadgets—not to mention toys—for our baby. The things we buy for our child determines our effectiveness as parents. That's the message.

But it takes money to buy everything from the engagement ring to the house and car and baby paraphernalia. So what becomes number one in the life of the married couple? You guessed it—jobs and careers as means to the accumulation of money and possessions.

Husband and wife may continue to say that their marriage is most important for them, but their actions reveal their belief that marital happiness depends on things outside their relationship: jobs, money, and the accumulation of more and more material possessions. In the pursuit of greater affluence, many couples neglect the marital relationship.

A priest we know once told us of a young man who came to him with this account of his situation: "Father, Jane and I are getting a divorce. I just can't understand it. She has a job that brings in $40,000 a year. I make about $50,000. We have a big beautiful house, two cars, and a lake cabin. Last summer we took a vacation in Hawaii. Why is our marriage ending in divorce?"

Any married couple needs a certain minimum income, a decent place to live, and enough food to eat and clothes to wear. All of these require the regular appearance of paychecks. Unemployment or the lack of an adequate income can have terribly destructive effects on a marriage. But as Americans we always want more; we are never satisfied with what we have. We believe in our secret heart of hearts that the accumulation of ever more money and the attainment of a higher degree of affluence will lead to personal happiness.

We really do think that our marriage will be better once we have more money or a bigger house or a new car. We really do believe family relationships will improve once we don't have to watch our pennies so closely. The mistake is in acting as if the quality of our marriage depends on things outside the marital relationship itself.

To repeat, certain minimums are necessary: clothes, food, a roof over our heads. But how much do we really need to be happy? Very little, really, by typical American standards. If we stop to think about it, most of us have more than enough. It's time to shift attention to our marriage, to the continuing impact spouses have on each other. It is time to spend regular time on us, even—perhaps especially— if it means spending less time on the job or career.

Another tactic married couples frequently find convenient for avoiding one another is the children. We want to provide the children with all the things we never had. Or we feel guilty if we are away from the children when we could be with them. It is, of course, important for parents and children to have plenty of quality time together. But what kids need most is parents who have a healthy, happy marriage. There is a limit to the amount of time parents can spend with their children before they reach a point of diminishing returns, as it were.

One of the best things parents can do for their children—no matter what the ages of the kids—is to get away from them at least twice a month and simply enjoy each other. Spending time and some money on our marriage is important. Sacrifices will be necessary. Personally, we have spent more than a little money on evenings out and baby-sitters. This is money that we could have saved or spent on "nice new things." Instead, we continue to spend it on us, on dinners out, on movies we attend together, on plays we want to see or concerts we enjoy together.

Of course, money is not the point. A regular evening out together can be as simple as cups of coffee or hot chocolate shared together in a quiet cafe. The point is the time together away from the kids. The kids will benefit as much from this as we will. And when the kids are gone— which they will be far sooner than we think—we will still know each other, instead of being virtual strangers.

Marriage is not a static relationship between two static people. Marriage is a process or set of processes to which a man and woman commit themselves. Marriage is a woman and a man who promise to be there for each other. And so they must be there, not just physically in the same room for breakfast and dinner with the kids, but emotionally, psychologically, and spiritually, on a regular basis. They must be there with each other in an undivided way, to talk, to listen, to have some simple fun together once a week or so. After all, isn't this why people get married in the first place?

Don't be fooled. Time and discipline are necessary if we want to be sure that we have quality time together regularly. This means getting out the calendar and putting ourselves on it right along with the PTA meetings and the hours of volunteer work.

What it all comes down to is taking the trouble to be sure that the other person feels loved and not taken for granted. Someone said that the opposite of love is not hate but indifference. Thinking that we are taken for granted feels awful. Fragile beings that we are, we need to be reminded in ways we can feel that we are special, loved, valued, and cared for.

This is a great part of what married love is meant to be for Christian believers: the experience of God's love through the love of my spouse. I am meant to know the fullness of God's love when my spouse loves me in ways that help me to feel loved. My spouse can tell me about it—and words of love are important—but words alone tend to lose their power. He or she must show me; must use symbols and gestures. My spouse could bring me flowers; fix my favorite dinner even though it takes extra time and effort; take the kids to the park so I can have a quiet afternoon around the house; spend some money we can't afford to spend for some small gift he or she knows will speak a deep love for me.

To nourish marital intimacy is what a spirituality of marriage is all about. Sometimes this means that I must struggle to overcome the effects of past experiences that keep us from being closer. Perhaps my mother passed along to me feelings about my sexuality that make it difficult for me to experience the fullness of joy and pleasure in our sexual lovemaking. Maybe as a woman I don't feel as attractive to you as you say I am. As a man, perhaps I have a difficult time being anything but the aggressor when we make love. Or maybe I find it tough to be tender or to tell you about my fears and anxieties. I think I could overcome these negative residuals in myself that hinder our relationship, but I need your help—and I do not find it easy to ask for your help with something so personal, such a sensitive part of myself.

There is perhaps no more powerful way in which a married couple experiences the spiritual quality of their relationship than when they make love. In fact, however, sexual lovemaking is for the Christian couple a celebration of the sacrament of marriage. Spirit cannot be separated from body; bodily love cannot be separated from spiritual love.

So it is part of the discipline of a marital spirituality to love each other in every dimension of our relationship, to nurture our love with joy, passion, pleasure, and peace through sexual lovemaking. It is part of the discipline of a marital spirituality to strive to overcome anything which handicaps the full celebration and renewal of our relationship through sexual ecstasy.

Still another aspect of the discipline of a marital spirituality—an aspect which demands effort and persistence—is the need to learn effective intimacy skills. Here, of course, the topic is the broad-based intimacy which is meant to pervade every aspect of the couple's relationship. Every couple can use some renewal of their intimacy skills. It is a fact of modern life that no marriage can hope to weather the predictable and unpredictable events of a shared life without knowing how to communicate effectively. Couples must take the trouble to learn the practical skills that are available to them to facilitate communication rather than allow it to be a kind of hit-or-miss proposition.

Ideally, youngsters from their earliest days of formal education would be taught good communication skills. Couples who are married and who are getting married today have rarely learned the practical communication skills that are so important to the quality of their relationship. It is a part of a marital spirituality to learn these skills and to use them well.

Let's think back to when we were first going together. What was it about each other that we found most intriguing? What was it we spent so much time talking about? It was, of course, our individuality—our different interests, our unique perspectives on life, our delightfully special way of being just who we are.

It is highly beneficial to a marriage to keep this individuality alive, because it contributes to the growth of our relationship as a couple. There is no room for an attitude which would view one spouse as somehow incomplete without the other. A marriage is made by two complete individuals who are perfectly capable of being self-sufficient. Only then is the gift of self to the other possible, for only then do I have a complete self to give.

So it is nourishing to a marriage for spouses to give each other the time to pursue individual interests and enthusiasms. Each couple will have a balance of together and individual time that fits the unique character of their marriage. But both need to be there. By continuing to be alive and to grow as an individual, I can keep myself interesting for my spouse. For one thing, this will continue to provide us with new topics for discussion. This is also a practical way of keeping in mind that I can never know completely the constantly changing, fascinating mystery that is my spouse. Instead, the adventure of discovering each other goes on for a lifetime.

The Christian married couple also shares a life of prayer. Some couples find that even sexual intimacy is not as personal as one's prayer life. For a couple to share prayer in some fashion is to share a dimension of their relationship where the mystery of being called together by God becomes almost tangible. Words become inadequate, perhaps.

Maybe the best form of shared prayer for the Christian couple is shared silent prayer. When husband and wife sit or stand or kneel together in prayer and each speaks silently to God the deepest thoughts of his or her heart, at that moment the intimacy of the couple is impossible to describe. When wife and husband share spontaneous spoken prayers, there is always the possibility of feeling the need to "perform" for one's spouse or to meet unspoken expectations.

Regardless of how a couple prays together, however, to make times for praying together is to allow for space in the marriage for the Spirit to speak out of the needs and joys of the marriage to the loving God who nourishes the relationship of the couple in real, but hidden, ways.

Finally, there is a need to speak at least briefly about roles in a Christian marriage. This is a topic that has many significant implications for the ways in which a Christian marriage is lived from day to day.

An older understanding of marriage viewed the relationship between husband and wife as basically authoritarian. In this view, the husband is "head" of his wife. He makes all the important decisions, although he may likely consult with her. The wife, for her part, bows to the authority of the husband in matters important to the marriage and the family. For social and cultural reasons, since the nineteenth-century Industrial Revolution, this has also meant that the husband was the "breadwinner" and the wife the "homemaker" and primary nurturer of children.

This older understanding of roles in marriage sometimes gains justification from a fundamentalist interpretation of the Bible. This perspective leads to a "headship" and "submission" model of marriage. Drawing upon certain Old and New Testament texts, fundamentalist preachers and teachers insist that in the biblical scheme of things, the husband must exercise "headship" over his wife. The wife, in turn, must be submissive to the "headship" of her husband as her way of relating to Christ. By being submissive to her husband, the wife submits to the will of God in her life.

Fundamentalist Christians maintain that this interpretation of the Bible is God's will for marriage. Today a few Catholic biblical fundamentalists choose to do the same. In essence, they teach that a couple cannot have a truly Christian marriage unless they practice the headship/submission model of marriage provided for by a fundamentalist interpretation of Scripture.

The only support for this opinion is the fundamentalists' own interpretation of the Bible plus, in a few instances, attempts on the part of Catholic fundamentalists to dredge up what they perceive to be data in support of their position from the social sciences. Nothing in the official teachings of the Catholic Church states that a couple must practice headship and submission. Catholic Scripture scholars overwhelmingly reject the notion that the headship/submission model is the only one acceptable for Christian couples. Numerous statements by Pope John Paul II would, if anything, lend support to a marriage based on the fundamental equality of husband and wife:

> When St. Paul wrote that "wives should be submissive to their husbands as to the Lord," he did not mean that the husband is "boss" of the wife and the interpersonal pact of matrimony is a pact of dominion of husband over wife. There is to be no one-sided domination. Each is to be subject to the other from a sense of Christian piety.

Our own conviction is that it is possible to have a Christian marriage and base that marriage on any number of models insofar as roles are concerned. To one degree or another, most couples marrying today seem to prefer a model that presumes the basic equality of wife and husband. There is rarely any strong sense that the husband is endowed by God with a superior form of authority. This is called a two-vote rather than a one-vote marriage. When important decisions must be made, husband and wife collaborate.

This "companionate," or two-vote marriage, frees husband and wife to relate to God through one another equally. The husband is submissive as often as the wife. Couples work out the practical details of generating income, cleaning the house, doing the laundry, caring for children, and preparing meals in ways with which both are comfortable. But they take for granted their basic equality as persons. They understand that all practical arrangements in the daily living of marriage and family life are open to renegotiation at appropriate times.

Each marriage is unique because two unique individuals live it. Every married couple has the right to develop an understanding of roles in marriage that works best for that particular couple. Wives and husbands are free to agree on a headship/submission style of marriage if they wish. Other couples should feel no constraint to do likewise if they prefer a companionate style of being married Christians.

We began this chapter by pointing out that the married couple constitutes the smallest form of church—a form of church which is authentic, not just a living analogy or metaphor for "real" forms of the church. By nourishing the ongoing intimacy of their relationship according to gospel values which place love of God and neighbor at the heart of married life, the couple faithfully respond to their vocation to be a healthy and nurturing basis for the home church that is their family.

THE SEXUAL, SPIRITUAL FAMILY

Chapter Five

$\mathcal{W}$e are sexual beings. From his or her basic genetic structure on out, each person is either male or female, and our sexuality conditions our entire being. Each thought, word, and action is that of a male or a female person. It is impossible to be in the world except in a sexual way.

At its most fundamental, our sexuality constitutes our capacity to be in relationship with other persons in more than a superficial fashion. Our sexuality enables us to be caring, other-centered, loving people. The woman or man who is psychologically or emotionally alienated from her or his sexuality is handicapped in the pursuit of human intimacy.

Thus, if we learn as children that our genitals are "not very nice" and that sexual pleasure is something to feel guilty about, we are crippled in our ability to be warm and loving with other people. On the other hand, a high level of comfort with our sexuality and with our body in general contributes much to our ability to be in relationships with others successfully.

Even our relationship with God is sexual, at least from the human side. God, of course, is "Person" in ways that transcend sexuality. Yet all the same, by way of the analogies of religious language, God is both female and male . . . and neither. Words of John Paul I, who died in 1978 after only a month as pope, are relevant: "God is a Father, but even more a Mother." Apart from spiritual schizophrenia, we cannot set aside our sexuality, not in our relationships with other men and women, not in our relationship with God.

Sexuality has a profound impact on family relationships too. On the ways we understand our roles in the family and the ways in which we communicate Christ to one another. The family is a complex network of sexual relationships which, when examined from the perspectives of our religious tradition, reveal the presence of the Creator in whose image we are created.

Femaleness and maleness, then, are much more than biology. They are more than a psychic reality. Because our sexuality is part of "everything that [God] had made," it is "very good" (Genesis 1:31). The implications of our sexuality for the life and spirituality of a home-church are important ones. For the mystery at the roots of human sexuality draws a man and a woman together. This mystery, which is the origin of their faithfulness to one another in love, enables husband and wife not only to witness to but to participate in the making of babies and in the decades-long process of giving birth to new human persons.

Indeed, sexuality is a primary source of the bond between spouses, and it is sexuality—the capacity to touch others with love and to be touched by them in return—that draws the young gradually away from their family of origin into the formation of new, loving relationships and new families of their own. If it were not for human sexuality, none of this would happen, except perhaps as it happens for cats and monkeys, birds and fish.

What does being a woman mean? What does being a man mean? How can female and male persons be in relationship with one another in ways that are most fully human? How can men and women be in relationship with members of their same sex in ways that do justice to the human mystery?

If we are to understand the role of human sexuality in the spirituality of a family, questions like these are of basic importance because love for one another is central to the purpose of a family's existence and central to the Christian meaning of life. Let us begin to do this, if only in an incomplete way.

Nothing has had so profound an effect on the self-awareness of both women and men in the final decades of the twentieth century as the movement among women to transcend the ways in which society, culture, and history defined women and their roles. Some activists in the women's movement formulate goals that not many can agree with. But in great part, the women's movement leads in directions which have beneficial effects on the lives of women, men, and society as a whole.

Families are in a position to benefit from female and male images which develop as a result of the women's movement. Christian families in particular may benefit from these new images because, on a practical level, they can help family members relate to one another in ways consistent with the spirit of the gospel and with the teachings of both the Old and New Testaments. Christian feminist scholars present ample evidence that feminism and Catholicism can benefit from a dialogue based on based on mutual respect. Thus, listening critically to the women's movement from a Christian perspective can greatly enrich the life of a Christian family.

Down through the centuries there is probably no institution with which women have been so closely associated as the family in its various forms. Yet the specific ways we have come to view this association are no older than the Industrial Revolution. Prior to the emergence of the assembly line, "sweat shops," and white and blue collar work, the place of women in families was far different from what it was by the time today's married couples were growing up. The radical division of roles and labor between the home and the workplace had not occurred. Home and workplace—typically a family farm— were for most people one and the same.

With the triumph of the industrial system, however, factories and offices enjoyed great social status as the place where "the wheels of industry turned" and as the source of the family's income—while the home and the women who found themselves there were devalued. A "cult of domesticity" developed which was intended to salve the smarting self-image of wives and mothers and help justify the male abandonment of home, hearth, and family for the rigors of "the world."

The "cult of domesticity" glorified the home, maternity, and "wifely duties" in a world where everyone knew that what really mattered happened in factories and other workplaces dominated by men. Although male hats might be symbolically held over the heart at the mention of home, mother, and apple pie, those same hats would go back on as men agreed that "women's work" could not be terribly important. After all, it did not result in money, did it?

Women—confined to their roles as wife and mother—were placed on pedestals on the one hand but treated like children on the other. Men drew much of their self-esteem from being able to say, "My wife will never need to find work outside the home because I'm a good provider." By and large, middle-class women accepted the cult of domesticity since it became, in practical terms, their only source of self-esteem and . . . a very real source of domestic power.

While this sketch depends in great part on stereotypical concepts, it still faithfully reflects the main outlines of the worlds of the majority of men and women not so many decades ago.

One of the primary consequences of the women's movement is that more women today view marriage and family as one choice that is open to them. Not the only choice, just one of them. No longer is there a quasi-universal sense that the only choices open for Catholic women are marrying and rearing children or becoming a nun.

Even when women choose marriage and family—as most women do—few have much sympathy for the belief that a woman can be defined totally in terms of marriage and motherhood. Fewer Catholic women today expect their entire adult life to be taken up by full-time mothering, cooking, cleaning, and doing the laundry, with some volunteer work on the side.

We are at a stage of history where many women who continue to work outside the home after marriage also find themselves with primary responsibility for child care and domestic duties. Many husbands applaud the added income from their wife's job or career but still expect to relax at home while "the little wife" cooks dinner and changes diapers. Thus, we have the phenomenon of the woman with two full-time jobs—one as homemaker and another as secretary, waitress, business executive, or bus driver. Some women cooperate with this unfair arrangement for reasons of their own. Others become dissatisfied with it, and a marital crisis quickly develops.

We must uphold the right of each married couple to develop together their marital and family roles in ways best suited for them. But it may be that, in the not-so-long run, husbands and wives will discover that the more a relatively equal balance can be worked out, the more satisfying will their experience of marriage and family life become. For many couples, there may be something unhealthy about marital roles that isolate wives and husbands from whole areas of each other's daily life.

Ideally, men and women both need to be free to participate in the financial support of the family, and both need to be free to take responsibility for the physical maintenance of the home. Both spouses have a right to participate in the world of the workplace and of the wider society if they wish. Both can bring the Christian spirit to this arena in effective ways. Both have a right to the challenges and satisfactions of caring for children.

This may indeed be the ideal today. Yet relatively few couples find it possible to strike such a balanced bargain. Many employers resist arrangements that would free spouses to share careers or jobs and domestic and parenting duties on a fifty-fifty basis. This is but one way in which the lip service given to family life by politicians at election time and by corporate employers whenever convenient shows itself for the empty talk it is.

Many men still object to abandoning their (now illusory) role as "breadwinner," and many women cling to an image of themselves as "queen of the kitchen," even though they, too, work outside the home and "win" as much "bread" as their husband. But this is a transitional situation which may not last long.

The future may well see more and more families whose life will be characterized by a more-or-less equal sharing of roles, both inside and outside the family circle. Regardless of the specific arrangements worked out by individual couples, we will gradually discover new meanings in the words of St. Paul that in Christ "there is no longer male and female; for all of you are one in Christ Jesus" (Galatians 3:28). And this will lead to healthier marriages and happier families.

Moving toward this more balanced sharing of responsibilities is a vital element in a marital spirituality. Couples who have already taken steps in this direction readily admit that they are happy with sharing financial and domestic duties equally and that this has had a positive effect on their marriage, as well as on their effectiveness as parents. One wife commented:

> Our marriage is better in every way. We understand each other's joys and problems better, both at home and in our jobs, because we've both been there. We both feel that our need for work outside the home and our desire to be with the children and to putter around the house are being met in a balanced way. We now have a happier sex life too. And our kids like having more equal time with each of us.

Of course, there is a "down side" when both spouses work outside the home. Especially when they are very young, children do not receive the same care from nonparental caregivers as they would receive from a parent. Daily upkeep of the home may not be the same when both parents are absent, and meal preparation becomes a bigger challenge, sometimes giving way to sending out for "fast foods," such as pizza or hamburgers. Still, we must admit that many families have little choice because they find that the employment of both parents is economically unavoidable.

To overcome outmoded prejudices about women's and men's roles requires courage and trust that can come, for Christian men and women, from a lively faith. Faith comes to life when we take real risks with our spouse, with our sense of self, and with our expectations of married life and parenthood. This is one way in which a spirituality for married people jumps the gap from theory to real life.

Men, of course, often find themselves presented with unique challenges in the midst of society's questioning of traditional roles in families. What does being a man mean? A father? A husband? These are questions easily answered thirty years ago, but today, even men who cling to the old answers do so only under siege.

Psychologists tell us that both men and women have a "male" and a "female" side. Women, in order to be most fully what God created them to be, will sometimes act in what are typically recognized as "male" ways. Men, to be all God intended them to be, will sometimes be receptive and nurturant, behaviors traditionally identified with women. Yet women will be masculine in a feminine fashion, and men will nurture children and caress their wife, will let the feminine side of themselves come out, in masculine ways. In other words, both sexes experience the mystery of human sexuality in distinctive ways.

One of the greatest challenges to the modern male is the challenge to regain his feminine, nurturant, caring, sensitive, compassionate side, where emotions and feelings belong with "being rational" and where cuddling a child is as normal a male behavior as being an aggressive—or passive—lover with his wife. For today's "real man," the cultivation of family relationships takes priority over cultivating a wildly successful career. Giving himself to those he loves is more important than giving them an ever more affluent lifestyle.

Underlying the issue of sex roles in marriage and family life are two distinctive but complementary spiritualities. As mentioned early in this chapter, our sexuality conditions even our relationship with God. So there is a feminine spirituality and a masculine spirituality—womanly ways of being in the world in faith-filled ways and manly ways of doing the same. Heavily conditioned by society and culture though these are, they are nevertheless important to be aware of, to encourage, reform, and shape in ourselves according to the spirit of the gospel. Let us examine some of the possible characteristics of these male and female spiritualities.

A woman's spirituality is strong, resilient, and practical. It is rooted in the earth and in a natural communion with the One who gave birth to creation in the beginning and who nurtures it into existence during every moment of time. A woman's spirituality is interior and receptive, being open to the lover God in those she cares for and in the contemplative mystery of conception, pregnancy, and birth. Yet this female spirituality clings fiercely to the God to whom it is open and receptive and will not let go until it is graced by the divine power, though it take the patience of Job.

A woman's prayer is never cold. Always it is passionate, even when it is dry or seems to echo with only a great Absence. This is a spirituality familiar with the need to labor by cooperating with the Creator's labors in a woman's life and in the lives of those she loves. A woman often knows when in life to get out of God's way as She labors and when to get pushy with God, insisting on some action.

A woman's spirituality sees signs of God in human emotions and naturally employs the nurturing, empathetic, relational qualities with which a woman is often gifted. A woman's spirituality may easily grasp the importance of bringing these qualities into the world of the workplace, and the world of the church, dominated for so long by a masculine spirit out of touch with its own feminine dimensions.

What of a masculine spirituality? It is insistent but gentle, in love with the lover God as a man with a maid. Male spirituality marches up to the dwelling-place of God and bangs on the door when the lives of those a man loves are at stake. A male spirituality is contemplative in its activism. It knows that its roots are in the world of the family, so this spirituality is oriented toward the building of familial relationships.

A masculine spirituality actively pursues intimacy with wife and children, tosses life in the air like an infant, and plays with the Spirit as if She were a child. A masculine spirituality, full of laughter in the face of an uncertain future, refuses to take Mammon too seriously. The spirituality of a Christian man understands that work has value in itself but that work, in the end, is for life, not the other way around. A masculine spirituality brings a Godly spirit to the world of jobs and careers.

A masculine spirituality is modest and devoid of self-righteousness. It rejoices in the beauty of the feminine but says, "I pass" when the world would make of women mere objects. A masculine spirituality knows that to make women objects is to deal a wicked blow to the integrity of self and to the goodness of the Creator of women and men.

If these feminine and masculine spiritualities look as if they are not so distinctive after all, that is because they overlap and commune one with the other. This is another characteristic of both: They seek each other in order to be complete. Each drinks from the other's well.

Have we strayed from our theme of family spirituality, of ways for the home church to live according to the gospel in the modern world? Not at all. For an essential element of family life is its role in forming men who are genuinely masculine and women who accept and celebrate their femininity in all its dimensions. A family spirituality includes the discipline of enabling husbands and wives, girls and boys, single mothers and fathers to live as the fully sexual beings God thinks it is good for them to be.

In our family we respect and rejoice in maleness and femaleness to the point that sometimes we seem to take sexuality for granted. We don't pretend that human sexuality is either unimportant or the ultimate fact of life. Neither do we suggest, by word or deed, that we should fear or avoid talking about human sexuality or the human body. We laugh about human sexuality about as often as we speak of it with a straight face.

In the family, we learn that our sexuality—the gift of being able to care for and love others, the gift of being able to bring others into the comedy, the tragedy, the grand party that is life—enables us to be a family. Because of our sexuality we can be faithful in our love for one another and in our love for God who is Mother, Father, and Lover to us all.

CHRISTIAN PARENTING

Chapter Six

$\mathcal{B}$y virtue of their baptism, all Christians are called to service, that is, to serve others with the compassion, care, understanding, and joy of the risen Christ. Each is commissioned by Christ to bring the love of God to others in ways they can feel.

But we live in a world that frequently discourages the kinds of relationships between people that Christian service is all about. More specifically, the world of the workplace often urges people to look at one another as objects, while those who are parents are expected to be warm and caring at home.

Many people today sense a disparity between their understanding of themselves as disciples of Christ sent to care for others and their experience of a highly technologized and impersonal workplace. Not infrequently today, women and men work at jobs which result in their feeling like little more than extensions of a mechanical or electronic machine. The sense of alienation such people feel in relationship to their jobs is intense. Such people make up the rather high percentage of the workforce in some areas of the marketplace who turn to drugs—including alcohol—to help ease feelings of meaninglessness.

One example comes from a young woman who works as an information operator for a telephone company. During every minute of this young woman's on-the-job time, she provides anonymous voices in her headset with information about telephone services. Not only that, but the company this woman works for urges its information operators to keep their discussions with callers as brief as possible.

Our friend's average contact with a customer is twenty-seven seconds, but the company encourages her to get her average time down to twenty seconds. The ideal seems to be for the operator to become as "efficient" as the computer on which he or she punches buttons in order to locate telephone information for callers. Heaven forbid that the operator should encourage any kind of—even brief—human interaction. No. The ideal is to function with mechanical efficiency, even in contacts with human beings rather than computers.

This is but one example. Many others exist. But the problem is the same: human relationships and personal forms of interaction have little value. Even a company which proselytizes its customers to "reach out and touch someone" preaches the exact opposite to its employees.

What does this have to do with Christian parenting? It illustrates two sides of the same coin. First, we live in a world that does not truly value interpersonal relationships. Second, this is the world in which Christian parents try to nurture their children. This is the world many parents must live with during the many hours they work outside the home. This workaday world has an effect on our attitudes toward one another, even in our families.

Parents need to be aware of the ways in which human relationships during work hours may carry over to relationships in the family. Then we can support efforts to humanize the workplace. Moreover, we can be cautious in allowing employer attitudes about human relationships to dictate our attitudes toward relationships in the family. Through our family relationships we can remain sensitive to the need for warmth in human interaction, to the need to avoid treating others—even over the phone—as objects.

Within this social context, Christian parents are called to care for and guide their children. In this world, parents are called, in fact, to be the pastors of the home-church that is their family. The world does little to make the ministry of parents easier. But parents can be aware of exactly what kinds of "games" their society asks them to play. On the one hand, they can resist those games which would dehumanize family relationships. On the other, they can dedicate themselves to positive efforts to help children learn to be critical of such attitudes toward human relationships as we examined above.

Perhaps the main characteristic of Christian parenting is the understanding on the part of parents that they are called to parent in a faith context. Many of the forms of knowledge and the skills that are helpful to any parent are equally helpful to Christian parents. Christian parents have no magic formulas for raising children, no easy ways out of the tight spots all parents find themselves in with their youngsters from time to time. What especially characterizes the Christian parent is the religious values that provide a basis for the minor and major decisions that parents must make regularly.

One of the consequences of this faith context is the way the parent views the child. The Christian parent understands the child to be free, a gift, and a child of God. Let's examine each of these ideas separately.

The child is free. Of major interest here is the ways parents understand the nature of their relationship to the child. A more conventional way to approach this issue would be to raise the topic of parental authority. What exactly is the nature of the authority parents have with respect to their children? It is an authority that guides the child toward responsibility, self-reliance, and a mature adulthood.

The child is free. It is the task of parents to guide the young person as he or she develops and to help him or her learn to exercise that freedom responsibly. An earlier generation conceived of parental authority as meaning that when Dad or Mom commanded, children were to obey, whether they liked to or not. Today, it seems more appropriate to think of the task of parents as helping children learn to make choices and decisions of their own and of being with the child through the consequences which follow, be they pleasant or unpleasant. This is one of the most important ways parents can provide guidance toward independence.

This drive toward independence becomes particularly strong during adolescence, and parenting teenagers is almost always a major challenge. Few parents are lucky enough to have teenagers who breeze through their teen years with no major rough spots, no rebellion, no times very painful to both parents and kids. During the teen years, parents sometimes wonder at the sanity in having children at all. Why are they so disrespectful? Why do boys use language a sailor wouldn't use? Why do girls hold grudges? Where did we go wrong?

Maybe the best book in the whole world for parents of adolescents is *Parenting Teens with Love and Logic* by Foster W. Cline, M. D., and Jim Fay. (See suggested reading list at end of book.) Because we don't have the space to go into parenting teens in depth, we suggest that parents of teens read this book. We promise you'll be *very* glad that you did.

Briefly, parenting teens often comes down to a need to let the young person make choices and learn from the consequences. This can be difficult for a parent to do. But happen it must, sooner or later. We can wait until the teen finishes high school and leaves and let him or her do it alone, or we can allow the process to begin now, while the teenager is still living at home. Which do you think is the safer alternative?

As with most aspects of parenting, of course, it is our feelings and attitudes as parents that require attention first. Instead of looking at the child first, parents need to ask themselves some basic questions throughout the child-rearing years: Am I willing to facilitate my child's growth toward independence in reality and not just in words? Or do I grudgingly give up the power to control my child's life? Who am I protecting? Sometimes parents say they are trying to protect their children from serious mistakes when in reality they do all they can to protect themselves from the possible pain of watching their child suffer the sometimes cruel blows life can inflict, but which are often necessary for learning to take place.

Christian parents serve their children by nourishing in them growth in their independence or freedom as children of God. In this way, they acknowledge the second aspect of the child's identity: the child as gift.

In most families, the birth of a child happens so easily, so naturally, that the whole process of pregnancy and birth is accepted with hardly a second thought. It is easy to miss the sense of the child as gift, especially once the novelty of having a new baby around the house wears off.

But our children are unique gifts of God. They are sent to us, each as different from one another as are the snowflakes. Indeed, our children come, each in her or his own way, to help us grow up. It has been said that children make grown-ups of their parents. It is surely true that it is because of our children that we have the opportunity daily to do some maturing. This is one way to view the parenting task: If we do some growing up, so will our children. If we learn how to better live our lives, how to more faithfully follow Christ, how to more effectively respond to our children, then they, too, will grow up.

Our children are sent to help facilitate our growth as human beings. We sometimes forget that from the Christian perspective we experience self-fulfillment only by paradox. It is through death that we live. Sometimes it is through misery today that we know fulfillment tomorrow.

We feel sorry for ourselves. "Why have I been sent these kids who cause me so much anxiety, irritation, and trouble? Poor me." But in a very real sense, kids are only carrying out the commission (albeit unknowingly) given them by God. As an eleven-year-old boy remarked to his father, "Dad, don't you know that one of the reasons I'm here is to give you a bad time?"

Here we touch on an important aspect of a spirituality of parenting. Children—there is no getting around it—are one form the cross takes in the lives of parents. Because of children we have specific opportunities daily to die to selfishness, to sacrifice our most cherished prejudices, to set aside our preferences, and to ignore opportunities to coddle our own egos.

No monk rising from his bed of straw in the darkness of night to pray has more opportunities to die to selfishness than parents who rise in the night to care for a hungry or fussy baby or a child who is sick. This is dying to self for love of one's neighbor. No ascetic practices of fasting and penitence embraced by saints of old were more valuable in the eyes of God as ways to grow in love than the sacrifices made by parents to be able to spend more time with their children or to provide them with enough food or good schooling.

The parent who struggles to keep an open mind about his or her teenager's tastes in music and clothing strives to love in ways that cannot be measured. The parent who trusts a child a little more this year than last, and lives with the anxiety that comes with letting go just a little bit more, attempts to grow in her or his trust in God in ways that cannot be matched.

Third, the child is a child of God before he or she is a child of ours. As the *Catechism of the Catholic Church* notes, "Parents must regard their children as *children of God* and respect them as *human persons*" (no. 2222). Underlying the commitment to guide the child toward a responsible exercise of freedom, toward independence, is the firm belief that in the long run the child is in God's hands, not ours. We assent to the truth that this child is a mystery—known to us somewhat; known to himself or herself but incompletely; but known fully only by God. What greater cause for confidence, for hope, and for feeling okay about letting the child gradually grow up and away? As long as we do our best, we may trust that God can care for our children much better than we.

A traditional theological principle states that "grace builds on nature." Parents need to gain the practical forms of knowledge and the skills needed to be effective parents in today's world. On the "natural" level—prior to any consideration of the religious aspects of parenting—parents need to know their business. They need to ask the advice of experienced parents, read the books of the parenting experts, attend parenting classes, and join parent support groups.

All of this amounts to gaining practical skills. All the practical knowledge and skills the Christian parent gains become ways of showing God's love to the child in ways the child can feel. In these ways, love becomes real, not a matter of mere words and fond aspirations. As we relate to our children in the loving ways we learn, we observe in our own actions illustrations of how God loves us.

Parents can learn much about the love of God by paying attention to their own love for their children. Let's think of our own best moments of love for our offspring. That is but a shadow of how God loves us. Let's think of the times we let our child fall—literally or figuratively—in order for her or him to learn to walk. That is how God allows we to suffer a bit in order to grow stronger in spirit. Let's consider our feelings of pride and joy when our children are especially delightful. Just so is God's joy in our existence, our mere presence in the world of creation. This, too, is an aspect of a spirituality for parents.

Then there are the practical issues that fill a parent's days. To pick but two, let's examine the parent as educator in human sexuality and the parent as religious educator. As with every aspect of parenting, the parent is most effective in these areas if he or she first gains a balanced and mature integration of sexuality and of faith in his or her own daily existence.

Children begin learning about their sexuality and about relationships with members of the same and opposite sexes from the moment of birth. The baby that is fondled and caressed learns to relax and be comfortable with her or his body. The baby who has her or his hand regularly slapped when it happens to stray into exploration of her or his genitals will more likely have inappropriate feelings about sex to overcome in later years.

The child who witnesses his or her parents express warmth and affection for one another in physical ways—hugs, kisses, caresses—will feel loved because he or she is confident of living in a loving atmosphere. Such a child will also learn that physical expressions of love and affection are not only appropriate but to be rejoiced in.

Education in human sexuality and religious education have much in common. Both are—in the now widely used phrase—"more caught than taught." Kids pick up almost with the air they breathe their parents' feelings and attitudes about human sexuality. The same goes for religion and for the living of one's faith in daily life. Kids know when religion is little more than a formal exercise to be endured on Saturday evening or Sunday morning (even if parents never come right out and say so), and the most important part of sex education is parental attitudes toward sex.

Children also have a kind of sixth sense when it comes to parental attitudes which make of faith little more than a psychological security blanket instead of a constant challenge to take real risks based on faith and to embrace the cross on a daily basis, in all kinds of ways, for love of God and other people. Kids have an uncanny ability to recognize when parents are merely playing games with religion. They can spot phoniness in faith a mile away. They can also recognize authentic faith the minute they see it being lived in concrete ways. Kids reject phony faith on the spot; they are naturally attracted to authentic faith.

As religious educators, it is not the task of parents first of all to trot out religion books once a week and sit down with the kids to drill them. Neither is it their first obligation to enroll the children in a Catholic school or religious education program—worthwhile though either of these actions certainly is. Instead, it is the most basic responsibility of parents to do all they can to continually grow and mature in faith themselves. Do I look at daily life from the perspectives of the gospel or from the perspectives of the stock market? Which do I value more, the opinions of Madison Avenue or those of respected teachers in the Christian community? Do I make regular efforts to grow in my understanding of my faith? Do I include personal prayer in my day? Do we as parents cooperate in our efforts to help our children learn about and live the Christian faith?

What about our attitudes toward our relationships with our children? We may say that spending time with our kids is more important than buying them the latest styles in clothing and the toys and games that are currently being hyped on television. We may say that our children are more important to us than our jobs or careers, more important than our hobbies. But is this so?

One of the best ways to discover where our values really are is to look at our calendar and at our checkbook. Where do we spend our time and money? Do we spend more time making money in order to buy things for our kids than we spend simply being with them? Do we have a tendency to buy things for our kids to compensate for our failures to share ourselves with them?

When was the last time we took a financial risk for the sake of some enjoyable family time together? Oh, it is relatively easy to take a risk when a necessity is at stake—food, clothing, the rent, and so on. But what about taking financial risks for the sake of what is equally important—collecting memories we can share as a family, memories that will bind us together?

Irish political activist Bernadette Devlin wrote, in her autobiography *The Price of My Soul,* that she could always tell as a child when her parents were about to do something for family time together that they couldn't afford. She would hear them say, "There'll be days when we'll be dead."

Bernadette always knew that they were about to take a family vacation or weekend trip together for which there was no money. But her parents valued the short time of their life together more than possible—even likely—financial shortages. Somehow the money would work itself out. And it always did. Bernadette Devlin's parents believed in taking risks in order to put first things first.

Another aspect of sharing faith with our children that is frequently overlooked is introducing our kids to the whole church. Most kids grow up thinking that their parish church is all there is to being Catholic. Thus, they may never experience the rich variety that is the patchwork quilt of Catholicism. As kids grow up, they need to see up close a Catholic Worker House of hospitality. They need to spend some time around a Trappist monastery.

The child's perspective on the church can broaden considerably by attending Mass at various ethnic parishes. The sense of faith comes across in different ways at an inner-city parish potluck dinner than it does at a suburban parish picnic. Take them to hear the prayerful chant of a group of Poor Clare nuns. Introduce them to one of Jean Vanier's L'Arche houses where mentally handicapped persons and their assistants live together in Christian community.

In every part of the country there are different ways to be Catholic happening almost side by side. We can let the kids gain a feel for what Catholic means: universal. Let's try to include the Catholic "sights" along the way on our summer vacations too. North America is dotted with Catholic shrines and points of interest. We can make of these stops not just more rubbernecking on the part of tourists, but part of an authentic pilgrimage, an attempt to enrich the faith of our family.

So much of the impact parents have on their children happens through simply living together. One of the most profound forms of education children gain from their parents is the preparation they receive to form families of their own one day. Girls and boys learn how to go about being wives and husbands by the ways they observe their own parents doing this. They learn how to parent by being the subjects of parenting.

Of course, none of this amounts to a kind of absolute conditioning process. In later years, our offspring can often overcome inadequacies in themselves which may be due to our parental blind spots or failures. Nevertheless, it is almost impossible to overemphasize the impact parents have on their children when it comes to preparing them to be spouses and parents themselves in adulthood.

There is so much that can be said about parenting. Shelves and shelves of books on parenting fill libraries and bookstores. But when all is said and done, we believe Sidney Callahan states in an excellent and concise fashion the ultimate goal of the Christian parent: "to make our children glad they were born and eager for life." If we keep this objective in mind, no matter what the practical issue at hand, the approach best adopted by parents will become apparent soon. Living out of a faith perspective, the Christian parent is especially well equipped to accomplish precisely this goal.

Two-Parent and Single-Parent Families

_____

Chapter Seven

There are many single-parent families in Catholic parishes today. It is therefore imperative that a book on family spirituality give some attention to the experience of single parents and attempt to reflect on the unique dimensions of a spirituality for the single-parent family. At the same time, many of the issues single-parent families have are the same ones two-parent families must deal with. In this chapter, we will discuss some of the issues that arise from the fact that a family has one or two parents.

For many single parents, "single parenthood" is a phase which may last only a few years—between divorce, the birth of a child "out of wedlock," the death of a spouse and marriage or remarriage. For others, marriage or remarriage may not be a consideration for many years, if at all. Some single parents today eventually link up with another single parent to form the phenomenon of the "blended" family. This is a form of family which has unique characteristics, needs, and strengths, but which is beyond the scope of the present discussion.

The single-parent family is a true family and a legitimate form of home-church. For all the ways in which it is unique, it remains a genuine family, a small cell of Christian life. It is from this fact that the basic principles of a single-parent family spirituality will emerge.

It may be helpful, however, to first examine some of the special characteristics of the single-parent family. Both parent and children have gone through painful disruptions that marked the months, sometimes years, which led to a divorce. The family has survived, even though both parent and children have known much anguish.

Generally, it takes between two and five years for the practical and emotional aspects of life to settle down again. Sources of income must be developed, a move to a new house or apartment may be necessary, kids may need to attend different schools. Parent-child relationships must be redesigned. Raising children as a single parent is very different from doing so in tandem with a spouse.

The single father—usually, though not always, the noncustodial parent—struggles with a whole new set of difficulties. Often there is the need to pay child support to his former spouse. He may become deeply worried about the religious upbringing of his children, should his former wife remarry someone who is indifferent or antagonistic to Catholicism. The noncustodial father also typically has more time to become depressed. He may suffer from acute loneliness.

In fewer situations, single parenthood is the result of the death of a spouse. In such instances, the grieving process unique to this set of circumstances goes on for many months. Yet, as one divorced woman pointed out, the single parent who has been widowed has something going for him or her that the divorced person usually does not. The widowed parent tends to be looked upon by the wider community as courageous, as one who is "slugging it out through thick and thin," after the tragic death of a beloved spouse.

Even today, others often view the divorced Catholic parent with suspicion. In some parishes the single parent who is divorced often feels shunned, ignored, even subtly ostracized. Yet divorced single parents have a deep desire to belong, to be a part of their church and their parish. Single parents have a need for sympathetic friends and for warm relationships with "normal" two-parent families. Two-parent families need to remember that they have much in common with single parents, and they need to try to offer support and encouragement when possible. It is even likely that a single parent may have some insights that couples who are parents will find helpful.

In the majority of cases, the single parent is a woman. Usually she is divorced, although there is quite an increase in the number of young women who, after becoming pregnant while single, choose to raise their child as a single parent rather than place the child with an adoption agency. But in either case, the fact of being a single woman with family responsibilities is often seen as a handicap in our society. Women are not generally paid as well as men for similar work. They also have a more difficult time finding jobs that pay well in the first place.

The single parent, whether male or female, might be most accurately described as a survivor. Yet she or he is frequently not sure that the survival will last until the end of the week. All day long, the single parent responds to the demands of either children or employer, and she or he does it alone. If the single parent is lucky, there is an hour or two left over at the end of the day, after the kids are asleep, when the single parent can simply sit down and relax—or perhaps "collapse and relax" would be more accurate. This block of time, if the single parent is fortunate enough to have it, is critically important to the maintenance of some degree of emotional and psychological stability.

The same is true for couple parents, but they have the advantage of being able to relieve each other now and then. Sometimes husbands still think of their wives as the main parent, so they don't think to offer their spouse some relief. It takes a man and a woman to make a baby, and the male's responsibility does not end when the baby is born. It is only just beginning, and the sooner good old Dad accepts this the better off the child will be, the healthier his wife will be, and the healthier their marriage will be.

Weekends, for both single-parent and couple-parent families, are times for "catching up"—catching up with the housework, catching up with shopping for groceries, catching up on yard work, and taking care of errands that won't get done any other time. Of course, a parent may be required to work on weekends, in which case the disparity between the parent's schedule and that of the kids who are still in school further complicates matters. There is also the question of care for children during the summer when parents must continue to work but school is out.

Most single-parent families must constantly struggle with financial anxieties. Even if an absent father pays child support, the shift from being a two-income or one-male income household to a one (usually female) income household is typically traumatic. Even college-educated single mothers often find themselves seeking help from county or state agencies.

At the same time, financial stress is simply part of life for almost all families. As Dolores Curran wrote in her book *Stress and the Healthy Family*,: "When I began researching why money is such a debilitating stress, I presumed that *insufficient money* would be the cause, but I was wrong. While families often name lack of money as the culprit and assume that if they just had more, their financial pressures would go away, my research reveals that those in all income categories named money as a top stress—those with incomes over $40,000 as well as those with incomes under $10,000.

Probably the best word to describe the condition of the parents—single or couple—is *tired*. One single mother of two preschool-age children remarked: "I seem to be exhausted all the time, I never really seem to feel rested and relaxed. There just isn't time for that because it's push-push-push, all day long, every day." Again, the main difference for the single parent comes from having to cope alone.

Married parents get tired too. But there is something about being tired *with* another adult that makes it, by comparison with the single parent's tiredness, more bearable. In a two-parent family, Dad can take the kids to the park for the afternoon so Mom can relax for a couple of hours. In the single-parent family life isn't that simple.

Most single parents find that because they must give virtually all of their time to children and "bringing home the bacon," there is little time left over for keeping a clean and tidy house. Even those who consider themselves incapable of living in a "messy house" learn to live with the mess. It's unavoidable. One mother commented, "When you're a single parent, something has to go, and it's usually the upkeep of the house."

With all the time that must be given to caring for children, most of it involves taking care of essentials— preparing meals, helping with homework, getting children off to school in the morning and into bed at night. Single parents often feel guilty about not spending enough quality time with their kids. In a two-parent family, on Saturday Dad can prepare lunch while Mom reads the little ones a story or acts as a taxi service for older kids. In the single-parent family, if Mom is fixing dinner, that's it; there is no one free to read a story or simply listen to how school went that day. Mom is responsible for everything, but everything is not about to get done.

One of the deepest pains experienced by the single parent is the knowledge that, in the words of another single mother, "My children will never have witnessed a normal man/woman, husband/wife loving relationship. This leaves a great void in their lives, I think. This is the one thing, as a single parent, that I cannot give my kids."

While this parent's words have the ring of truth about them, it's no good to idealize two-parent families. Many children who grow up in two-parent families see in their parents' marriage less than the ideal. It's best if both single and couple parents do the best they can all around and let the chips fall where they may. No parent or set of parents can give children everything they should ideally have. We all have our limits, and it's only realistic to accept them.

Both single and couple parents operate at peak energy-expenditure levels day in, day out. Single parents are, however, perhaps more inclined to the "super parent syndrome." Now and then, a single parent decides that she or he is going to be super parent and may remark that her or his "kids aren't going to have it any different from other kids." Such a parent, in the words of a single father, "is setting himself up for two or three ulcers and a one-way ticket to the loony bin." The single-parent family is unique, and as we shall see, accepting this fact is one element of a single parent's spirituality.

On the other hand, single parents may have some advantages over couple parents. There is something to be said for being a survivor. Just "making it" is something to be proud of. In a society which often produces high school graduates who have never been required to take on responsibility for much more than school studies and maybe a part-time job, the children of single-parent families often find it necessary to grow up more rapidly.

Such kids are sometimes more mature than many of their peers from two-parent families. They have, of necessity, been trusted with significant responsibilities at home—everything from getting meals ready on time to shopping for their own clothes on a limited budget; from caring for younger siblings to making sure the car gets oil changes on schedule. In some instances, these kids *must* have part-time jobs, not to fund cars and stereo systems, but to contribute much-needed money to the family income.

Granted that this description of single- and couple-parent families is incomplete, it nevertheless reflects the general outlines of the parental experience. It is the real world of single and couple parents that is of prime concern if we are to reflect on the unique aspects of a spirituality of parenthood in these two unique yet overlapping situations. For, as we have said, an authentic Christian spirituality takes the real experience of real people and brings it into an intimate relationship with the gospel of Jesus Christ.

A spirituality for single- and couple-parent families does not lead into some dream world where there will be "pie in the sky by and by." Rather, it turns parents around to squarely face the realities of their life. This spirituality then enables parents to cope with these realities from a faith perspective—that is, from the perspective of a personal relationship with Christ. Single and couple parents who strive to be friends and follower of Christ confront the same facts of life as all parents. But they try to do so according to the perspectives of the gospel. It is this which makes all the difference.

The same gospel which is addressed to all challenges the single-parent family. But the response comes from within the unique circumstances of the single-parent family. Ditto for couple parents. They are called to respond to the gospel within the fabric of a two-parent family. Parents are called to conversion of heart and life, to trust God above all, to abandon fear, to love God and others as the source of life's meaning and purpose. Parents are called to do this even in the midst of meaninglessness and the temptation to despair.

As church, the single-parent family can cultivate prayer and family rituals, know forgiveness and reconciliation, cultivate a life of service, participate in a parish community, and proclaim the gospel effectively. If anything, the single parent may be more free to lead her or his children in this way of life. In two-parent families value conflicts which relate to the spiritual life of the family sometimes develop between husband and wife. Or one parent may choose to be a noncooperator with regard to fashioning the life of the family along explicitly Christian lines.

On the other hand, the single parent is free to provide religious leadership without possible hindrance from a reluctant spouse. The main prerequisite is the decision to live the life of a single-parent family according to the spirit of the gospel.

Single parents must often deal with two particular temptations: the temptation to self-pity and to resentment. The gospel challenges the single parent to leave self-pity and resentment behind. Support groups for single parents can be very helpful in the effort to overcome these self-defeating behaviors.

Couple-parent families must sometimes deal with the temptation to leave the main responsibility for parenting to the other spouse. Men, in particular, sometimes consciously or unconsciously believe that the woman is the primary parent. In today's shifting culture, this is no longer a realistic assumption. Unless each parent takes 60 percent of the responsibility for parenting, the marriage itself will suffer.

The difficulties unique to the experience of the single parent are very real, and the same is true for couple parents. But any life involves suffering. Every Christian is called to shoulder the cross in various ways, for it is only by doing so that authentic resurrection will ever be known, in this life or the next.

Single parents often have low self-esteem. But look. A single-parent family is still a family. We can be together each evening for dinner; we can join hands around our table for prayer. All it takes is the decision to try. We can still live our life together according to our Christian faith and strive to ignore the phony gods of a secularized society. All it takes is the ongoing decision to try to do so.

All families know insecurity. Many single-parent families are privy, however, to degrees of fear and anxiety that the typical couple-parent family does not usually know with such intensity. Financial anxieties may head the list, but a vague, undefined fear of what the future may bring is not far behind. The single parent is unable to share these fears and anxieties with another intimately known adult, and she or he lives with these feelings constantly. So the fear tends to compound itself.

All parents are called to turn away from fear and anxiety as motives for action. Parents can know that by dying to such fears even now they can know eternal life. Words of Jesus take on a special meaning for the single parent who may be anxious or fearful: "Fear is useless, what is needed is trust" (Mark 5:36). At the point that problems continue to pile up, parents can learn to let go and trust in God from deep within themselves. This is where faith is lived, in the real world.

In the two-parent family, it is crucial for spouses to spend time regularly on themselves and on their friendship as a couple. It is equally important for the single parent to carve out of the week a few hours for leisure and, now and then, for prayerful reflection.

Single parents may support one another in this. You take my kids on Saturday morning; I'll take yours on Sunday afternoon. Sometimes if the single parent's own parents or siblings live nearby, they can help her or him to have some regular leisure time. Two-parent families who are friends of the single-parent family are in a prime position to share their resources by offering supplemental child care now and then.

The single parent often finds it necessary to struggle against the tendency to become isolated. Parish community and support groups for divorced Catholics and single parents can be helpful. Isolation has its own unique dangers for the single-parent family, including the inclination to "make mountains out of molehills." That is, relatively minor difficulties can grow in the imagination until they seem completely overwhelming.

Single parents often need little more than a sympathetic listener, and they can frequently find this by forming friendships with other single parents and by membership in parish family groups. To have close relationships with two-parent families is often of special importance. Sadly, many parishes have still not grown to the point where family groups exist, and when they do, they are often at loose ends when it comes to welcoming single-parent families into their midst.

Not that couple parents don't need support, as well. Far from it. Parents in general often need other parents to simply commiserate with, to talk to and share their burdens and joys with. We should never underestimate the value of honest talking and listening among peers, for it is a terrifically valuable service that too often parishes do not offer to parents.

Continued faith in God and continued faith in oneself and in one's essential value constitute a constant struggle for many parents and make a real difference in how life is lived. We do not live in a world that values the contributions of parents. To go on believing that God's love is at work in my life as a parent and in our family relationships is rarely easy. But it is vital to keep on trying. A basic principle for a parent's spirituality is to "keep on keeping on."

The single parent who is widowed may recall that in the New Testament, we have witness to the compassionate love of Christ for the suffering of a widowed parent. Note that Jesus reaches out to help the woman without being asked to do so. Perhaps the woman's grief was so intense that she didn't know Jesus was there:

As [Jesus] approached the gate of the town, a
man who had died was being carried out. He
was his mother's only son, and she was a widow.
. . . When the Lord saw her, he had compassion
for her and said to her, "Do not weep."

Luke 7:12–13

Jesus looks with love on the pain of the widowed
parent and spontaneously reaches out to help. "Do not
weep," he says. Yet it is so easy for parents—couple parents
or parents made single through the death of a spouse,
divorce, or having never been married—to disbelieve this
love in their own life, to act as if parenthood somehow
casts us adrift from the love of God.

But even when parish communities are not as
supportive and caring as they should be, parents are never
alone. The caring and powerful love of God is there, and
the members of the family are given to one another as
signs of love by a loving God. Christ extends his hand and
invites parents to trust, even to trust blindly.

In the midst of our discussion, we must still be on the
offensive against misunderstanding, particularly when with
regard to the use of the term spirituality. Single and couple
parents sometimes conclude that spirituality is a luxury for
which they have neither the time nor the energy. They
assume that spirituality is an activity one engages in during
times which are set apart from ordinary life, or perhaps it is
a set of emotions one cultivates in order to "feel spiritual."

We must repeat that spirituality, even for parents,
refers first to the ways we strive to go about being in the
world. Spirituality refers to a decision or a set of decisions
about how we will live and about the ways we can follow
through on these decisions. The values, standards, and

goals we embrace are at the heart of our spirituality—the "whys" behind the way we live and the things we do. Thus, Christian parents choose to be led by the Spirit, rather than being led around by the nose by self-pity, resentment, or the dictates of a consumer culture.

Perhaps the major influence which shapes the divorced or widowed single parent's spirituality is that divorce or death has severed the deepest bond she or he knew in life. So the single parent needs to refashion a bond with God, the source of a love which is perfectly trustworthy and always there.

The single parent, even in minor matters, must make decisions about the lives of her or his children which demand a great deal of trust in God. Should I allow my daughter to attend a slumber party? Is she old enough? To make such a seemingly ordinary decision can be anxiety inducing in the extreme when it must be made alone. An important element in a single parent's spirituality is cultivation of the ability to be honest with one's children about parental anxieties and cultivation of the ability to make decisions trusting that in the end these kids are more in God's hands than our own. Couple parents sometimes must deal, in such situations, with disagreement over what to do.

Today, parents should have more of an impact on parish life and be less taken for granted. Parents may discover that a significant aspect of their spirituality is prophetic in nature. Parents need to have their concerns represented on parish committees and advisory groups, from the parish council to the liturgy committee. The perspectives, needs, and sensitivities of single-parent and couple-parent families deserve to be taken into account on every level of parish life, from the rectory to the committee charged with responsibility for planning the parish picnic. Homilists often could be more sensitive to the realities of family life with children too.

Someone needs to speak up for families with children in the parish. Who better than a parent who can say, "I've paid my dues as a parent." A single parent knows what it feels like to be a single-parent Catholic. A couple parent knows the experience of working through conflicts with a spouse who has a different perspective on the religious education of children. Parents cope with the financial worries and the worries about kids growing up in a secular culture, and someone needs to speak up for those who are parents in the parish

At the same time, often the other side of these experiences is a growth in compassion for all who suffer and a freedom to rejoice with those who rejoice. Parents who become deeper, more mature persons through their experience of parenthood are prime candidates for bringing a responsible, compassionate perspective to all aspects of parish life.

The spirituality of couple and single parents is based upon and nourished by the real world of family life with children. In some respects this calls forth a unique spirituality. But this spirituality is one which, like any Christian spirituality, brings parents and their children into communion with God and one another as its primary purpose.

THE HOME-CHURCH AND THE PARISH CHURCH

Chapter Eight

$\mathcal{A}$ family's participation in the life of a parish, congregation, or local church heavily affects that family's spirituality—its dedication to living the Christian life in everyday ways. So it is important to discuss the relationship between the family and the local church.

When *church* is mentioned, nearly all Catholics think first of their local parish. This is understandable. For as long as anyone alive today can remember, the parish is what we have meant when we say church. But today we are rediscovering that the parish church and the home-church are interdependent. We can't have one without the other. In his book *Religion: A Secular Theory,* sociologist Father Andrew Greeley states the point concisely: "The family is a more important institution of religious socialization than the church. But, the church is still important."

For many generations, parishes took families largely for granted. Parishes took for granted that families would remain basically healthy, that familial relationships would, for the most part, weather hard times. Divorce was relatively rare. Families often lived in places not too distant from grandparents, aunts, uncles, and cousins.

Parishes rarely doubted that family values would be shaped primarily by the Judeo-Christian tradition if not entirely by the church, at least through the vague but still identifiable and generally accepted manifestation of this tradition in society at large. Parish leaders knew they could count on Catholic families to support their parish, personally and financially. So, prior to about thirty years ago, few gave it a second thought. God was in heaven and all was more or less right with the world, the parish, and the family.

But the world changed, families changed, and parishes changed. Parish leaders can no longer assume that families will be more-or-less capable of nourishing the Christian life in their homes. Many families are terribly strained; many families break under the pressure of a secular world.

In the late 1970s, the Administrative Board of the United States Catholic Conference pointed out that secular mass media—most notably television—influence today's families far more effectively than the church does. The materialism of the secular culture impacts the life of a typical American Catholic family far more heavily than the gospel of Jesus Christ and the teachings of the church do.

As a result, families often feel a kind of emotional and spiritual schizophrenia. Many families attend Mass most Sundays but tend to view their religion as set apart from the rest of their lives: God is over here on Sundays or Saturday evenings, and maybe here for grace before meals on those rare occasions when we sit down to a meal as a family. "The real world" and our real lives, however, take up the far larger chunk of our time.

The Gospels proclaim that authentic human fulfillment and peace are found through a radical commitment to God and to other people—especially our neighbors, those with whom we live most closely. But through no fault of their own, Catholic families often live much like the rest of society lives in the pursuit of more and more of everything: money, possessions, a newer and bigger house, two or three cars, more beautiful landscaping around the house, a boat, a snowblower, two or three television sets, and an automatic garage-door opener.

Although the Gospels proclaim and the church teaches that the purpose of life is love of God and neighbor, many mainstream American Catholic families tend to reserve talk about such for inconsequential situations. When the chips are down, as they are nearly every day, life is about the pursuit of emotional satisfaction and security through the accumulation of more money and more of the things that money can buy and there is no such thing as enough.

The parish today is largely missing the boat because many Catholic families are not vital cells of Christian faith, hope, and love. Because so many families do not live their Christian faith on a daily basis what goes on in parishes is largely a matter of going through the motions during the week and formal ritualism on the weekends.

This is not meant to imply, of course, that parishes are completely phony. Certainly, they do much good: the sick are visited, certain individuals struggle heroically to make the parish a genuine Christian community. But this usually involves a minority of people. In most parishes, the great majority of those on the census list show themselves only on Sundays and rarely speak to anyone else. These are the "anonymous Catholics," who may drop a little or a lot of money in the collection basket but are almost never involved in the parish as a community.

That brings up the crux of the matter: most parishes are not communities. They are "sacramental service stations," places to turn to nourish one's individualistic piety; a place to go, perhaps, when our marriage is on the rocks; a place to send the kids for Catholic school or religious education classes. For many Catholics, the parish is for Sunday Mass, for baptisms, weddings, and funerals. For some it is the place for "going to confession." When our life is struck by tragedy, we might visit with a priest, a man we have probably never talked with before on any but a superficial level. But that's about it. Most parishes are not communities. Many Catholics don't understand that being Christian brings one into membership in a community. Being a Christian is *not* a private project, something we do publicly once a week and at times like Christmas and Easter only for appearances' sake.

What is the purpose of this long-winded streak of negative talk? The purpose is simply to illustrate that, generally speaking, parishes are out of touch with families, and families are out of touch with parishes. Families and parishes need one another if either is to be an authentic form of Christian community. At this point in history, the ball is in the parish's court. Either parish leaders begin to take effective steps to evangelize families and nourish family life and the Christian life in families, or the day is not far off when we can kiss the church good-bye as a viable institution in the North America.

Most parish renewal programs are based on the assumption—unspoken though it is—that a parish is a gathering of individuals whose relationships with one another are incidental to what the parish is about. Such programs fail to grasp the vital truth that the most important reality in any individual's life is his or her personal relationships. The most important reality in life is the couple's marriage; relationships between children and parents; the friendship between children and their grandparents, even if the grandparents live hundreds of miles away.

It is within the context of close personal relationships that we have our most basic religious experiences. We cannot separate love of God and love for spouse, children, parents, brothers, and sisters. Parish renewal programs that miss this critical point do little more than stir up the water for a few weeks, because they do not enable people to grow closer to one another and to see that this is where God is.

Very often parish leadership personnel are ill-equipped to understand and nourish families. The idea of family ministry is often perceived as just another program, something else for the parish calendar, another reason to set up another committee. Nothing could be further from the truth. Family ministry is far more than that: it is a wholly different way of being a total parish community. Family ministry is first of all a set of values and attitudes that inform and shape every ministry in the parish, from visiting the sick to the parish school or the religious education program for children; from weekend liturgies to the quality of life in the rectory.

Family ministry says that all ministries must be relational ministries. In other words, no matter what the situation, the central focus must not be on the individual isolated from others. Rather, it is a person's intimate relationships that constitute the heart of the situation. We minister to the individual by ministering to his or her relationships with those he or she loves, or at least we take them into account. We provide baptismal preparation not by handing the parents some facts about baptism and their responsibility for raising the child as a Christian. Instead, we introduce the family as a whole to a more complete participation in the Christian community.

If the family is not already participating in a neighborhood family cluster community, we have a representative of that "mini-parish" visit the family members in their home to acquaint them with the group's purposes, meeting times, and so on. We facilitate the nourishment of the couple's marriage. We find out what kinds of support the single parent needs. We nourish relationships in that family in any way we can. In this way, the family has opportunities to become better prepared to pass along the Christian tradition to the infant to be baptized.

The parish does these things because as a parish we have said that no family can live the Christian life alone, that no family can raise a child as a Catholic if that family is isolated from other Catholic families.

This illustration implies an important point. Fundamental to the mission of the parish today is the formation of basic Christian communities within each parish. These family-cluster communities are not based on a kind of group introversion. They must be based on caring for and serving one another, on growing together in faithfulness to the gospel and to meet catechetical and liturgical needs.

In addition, the focus must be on supporting and celebrating one another as families. We must never forget that the most important influence on the faith of the individual in the basic community comes from his or her relationships with those with whom he or she shares life most closely. Marriages need to be sustained and enriched;

parents need to be supported; retired couples need to be involved; single people need to be welcomed.

Each family-cluster community, if it is to survive and thrive, needs a common form of serving others. There must be a shared commitment to helping engaged couples prepare for marriage; to providing hospitality for the families of prisoners; to working for justice and peace; to looking after elderly persons, to visiting the sick; to demonstrating a lived compassion for families going through the tragedy of separation, divorce, the death of a spouse, or struggling with the disease of alcoholism. Why not arrange for the married couples in a basic community to become qualified to serve as paraprofessional marriage counselors?

Each little faith community in the parish must be involved in some form of shared service. Some will serve in support roles, others will be involved directly. When all is said and done, it is this shared service to others that bonds families to one another. It is this shared meeting of the needs of others that builds community.

The ministry of parish leaders and professionals from diocesan agencies is to support the ongoing existence of these basic communities within the parish. The parish staff can become the administrators of, for example, a parish referral service. A young woman is in the hospital following a miscarriage. Mrs. Smith can visit her because she had the same experience, and her husband can visit the woman's husband. Perhaps they can get together as couples.

A family in the parish with teenagers is experiencing a lot of turmoil due to the involvement of one of their children with drugs. Another family that successfully worked through just this situation can help by listening, by being there, and by sharing their own experiences.

Mr. Johnson's wife died yesterday. Call Mr. Carlson, whose wife died last year, and ask him to visit with Mr. Johnson.

One of the most important roles of parish ministers is to facilitate ministries within the parish. Family ministry is not merely professionals "doing unto" families. More importantly, it is families ministering to one another in all kinds of ways. If they are to live the Christian life, families need other families. Parish ministers can help to make this happen.

Anthropologist Margaret Mead once suggested that governments should be as sensitive to families as they are to the environment. Before a major construction project begins, an environmental impact study must be completed to determine how the ecological balance will be affected by the proposed construction. Dr. Mead suggested that governments should require similar studies to learn what impact civil laws, policies, and programs will have on the lives of families. Do our tax laws, for example, help or hinder healthy marriages and families? Do the educational policies of our schools contribute to the well-being of families or add to their burdens?

This same approach could be of immense value to parishes that are serious about supporting families as cells of Christian life. Parishes should ask families: "How do the programs, services, and policies of our parish affect your life as a family?"

Of course, this question must be expressed in particular questions that apply to the many specific aspects of parish life. Let's look at a few examples.

In many parishes religious education still confines itself to programs that divide families into age groupings, that divide men from women, teenagers from children and adults, and adults from teens and children. Thus, the parish fractures the family instead of supporting and strengthening it. One result of this is the traditional parish religious-education program for children. Let's say that the parish poses the following question to families: "How does our religious education program for children affect your life as a family?"

More than a few families would have to admit that the common approach to religious education for children fails to nourish family life; indeed, that in many cases, it has an eroding effect on family relationships. Most children's religious-education programs fail to relate in any significant way to the child's membership in a home-faith community. Parents and siblings share the child's formal religious education experience in nebulous ways, if at all. This, in spite of the fact that many religious education programs provide a "family" segment the child is supposed to take home and complete with a parent.

The one-hour-per-week approach to religious education for children typically overlooks that family relationships are at the heart of the child's faith-development needs. Moreover, the class schedule is usually mismatched to family routines. Once a week, Mom or Dad must fit a car trip to the parish facilities into an already busy schedule. Parents in some cases may sit in the parish parking lot while they wait for classes to end. In spite of all the words from official church sources about parents being the primary religious educators of their children, this common approach to religious education for children reinforces the idea that parents have little of significance to do with the child's religious formation.

Very possibly, parental responses to this line of questioning would lead a parish to reassess the value of current religious-education programs, if nourishing family life is basic to the mission of the parish.

Another area of concern might be the quality of parish liturgies. The Saturday evening or Sunday morning Mass is the one time of the week in most parishes when the church touches families as families in a direct way. So the question might be: "Do parish Masses nourish your life as a family?" Some parents would say that the opportunity for Sunday Eucharist gives them new strength to commit themselves to building strong family relationships. Others might respond that Sunday Mass is a needed respite from the daily grind.

But how many families' responses would reflect an awareness of the Sunday Eucharist as a celebration of their life as a small Christian community? How many would say that the homilies touch their life as a family and help them to be more faithful to their identity as the Christian community of the home? Perhaps the responses to a question on liturgy would highlight the need to fashion homilies and Sunday Masses more attuned to the lives of families of all kinds, more sensitive to the place of the family as the foundational church.

Many more specific questions could be formulated on issues that touch both parish life and family life: "How does the physical arrangement of pews and other furniture in our church affect your experience of liturgy as a family? (Ask the parents of young children that one!)

"How does our parish scheduling of evening meetings and educational programs affect your family's time together?"

There are dozens of ways in which parishes touch the lives of families, for good or for ill. So it is critical today for parish leaders to be aware of how their practical decisions help or do not help families.

Personal relationships enter into the picture in other ways too. The relationships that exist between families and priests are of prime importance. If a parish is to be a family of families, then the parish priest is key. Priests must accept the many important implications of the truth that the family is the foundational church; that unless the Christian life is lived by families it will be handicapped in parishes.

Some priests need to reexamine the assumptions upon which our understanding of the parish was based for so long—that the parish is an institution the pastor must keep in existence, primarily by being a manager and fund raiser; that the proper spirituality for a parish is individualistic or privatized.

It may be difficult for some celibate priests to appreciate the role of families in today's church. Sometimes, not inhabiting the same emotional and spiritual world as families, he doesn't develop a sensitivity to the intimate, personal, relationship issues that are so critically important to the faith and lives of families. Such priests need to take to heart the observation of author Father Alfred McBride that celibacy is meant to be a way of drawing closer to people, not a means for distancing oneself from them.

A first step toward bringing priests into the life of families would be for family people to gently urge their priests to move from institutional to family ways of thinking and living. Families may be called today to reach out to priests, to do what they can to draw priests into their family lives.

We are not talking about the polite, put-on-our-best-behavior business of getting out the good tablecloth because "Father" is coming over for dinner. Instead, families may simply draw Father into the everyday world of diapers and teenagers; the first year of marriage; family squabbles; grandparents; family games and family prayer; the world of tossing the salad, taking turns, and sharing. We do not mean to oversimplify here. It is never easy to bring about this kind of clergy-family sharing. But we must begin and keep on trying.

Priests sometimes need families that will encourage them to drop in when the notion strikes; to join them for dinner at the last minute; to come along for summer vacations or weekend trips; to leave the Roman collar in the rectory; to kick off their shoes and just be themselves, no formal meetings or programs, no agenda, no priestly "image" to maintain. When that happens, of course, the priest must be prepared to have his lap occupied by giggling or tearful little ones; he must be open to becoming a hugger and tickler of two-year-olds and a friend and confidant of teens.

Priests, for their part, can make the rectory a more family kind of place. One simple idea would be to invite a different family over for dinner one evening a week. The priest could make this an informal affair by giving the cook the night off and making way for "Family Night." He could get Mom and Dad involved with helping to prepare dinner in the kitchen. The kids could play outside or inside and not worry about being still and quiet. The parish could invest in a high chair for the rectory dining room for families who have a baby and a booster seat or two for toddlers. Then the priest and the family members could have a good old family dinner, nothing fancy, the primary purpose of which is the nourishment of relationships between priest and family.

Priests have a responsibility to do what they can to help married couples and children feel more comfortable in their company. If the priest takes the risks necessary to share his real self and life with married couples, married couples are more likely to feel comfortable sharing themselves and their marriage with him. It's a two-way street.

When priests share the lives of families and families share the lives of priests, they get to know one another apart from artificial clergy-laity distinctions. Do Catholics want vocations to the priesthood? We'll get them when kids have a chance to get to know the priest as a real person, not just as a distant liturgical functionary or authority figure. Do Catholics want priests who deliver homilies that make sense to the folks in the pews? We'll get them when Father experiences firsthand how faith is lived, celebrated, and struggled with by families in their relationships with one another.

Parishes need strong Christian families because without them parishes are empty of life and meaning. Families need parishes because no family can live the Christian life in isolation. A family may knock itself out trying to be an authentic cell of Christian life, a real home-church. But if the parish isn't faithful to its role as a nourisher and celebrator of family life and a convener of groups of families, that family will be weakened in its efforts to pass along the faith to children and to live that faith authentically in today's world. Parishes need families, and families need their parish. It's as basic as that.

The Family Proclaims
the Good News

Chapter Nine

$\mathscr{I}$n his 1975 apostolic exhortation, *On Evangelization in the Modern World,* Pope Paul VI noted that all the objectives of the Second Vatican Council "are definitively summed up in this single one: to make the church of the twentieth century ever better fitted for proclaiming the gospel to the people of the twentieth century."

The family-church is in an especially good position to play an effective part in this mission of proclaiming the gospel in ways that are credible in today's world. For the ideals and values upon which the family is founded are precisely the ideals and values which so many people crave.

We live in a world which hungers for human intimacy and intimacy with God. In its own unique ways, yet in ways it shares with all of human history, our age gives witness to the timeless words of St. Augustine: "Our hearts are restless until they rest in thee."

The Christian family strives to live according to the spirit of the Gospels in the everyday world. By doing this, it proclaims that the meaning of life is found in a human intimacy which is inseparable from intimacy with God.

Even the most obvious aspects of the dominant consumer culture in our society reflect a fascination with and hunger for all that *family* represents. The language and images of family and of human intimacy are second only to sex in their power to sell things. To name but a few examples, advertisers use the word *family* in advertising campaigns for restaurants, photographers' studios, automobiles, travel agencies, office equipment, and theaters. There is something about calling a restaurant a "family" restaurant that appeals to people. One auto dealership put up huge, expensive lighted signs to announce that its showroom was not a showroom after all. It had become a family room!

Banks and insurance companies are especially adept at the use of human intimacy language to sell their services. Their advertising invariably includes words such as *trust, fidelity, caring, protection, friend*. One bank calls itself "the friend of the family." "Like a good neighbor," a well-known insurance company "is there."

The psychology behind the use of family and human intimacy language for commercial purposes is not difficult to understand. It is easy to imagine the voice of an advertising executive saying, "People want family, they crave close, warm human relationships, right? But they aren't getting them. Look at the divorce rate; look at how people don't trust one another anymore. Parents and kids are strangers to one another. People don't even know their next-door neighbors! So what we do is capitalize on people's desire for family and warm human relationships. We use the language of family and friendship to sell! We promise 'em warm family relationships if they buy a car or eat in a restaurant. We use images of people who really like one another to sell soft drinks and beer."

If this tactic didn't actually work, billions of dollars would not be spent each year to produce advertising of precisely this nature. We are attracted to cars, restaurants, and home video games by the suggestion that they will bring family unity and friendship into our life.

This illustrates that people today do have a deep desire for human relationships that are more than superficial. Ultimately what we all long for is the loving God who alone can satisfy the thirst for the Infinite with which we are created. This is why the ordinary Christian family can be such a powerful agent in the proclamation of the gospel.

Through its life together, the family gives witness to the fulfillment to be found by those who seek human intimacy and intimacy with God. This is what the Christian family-church is about. The Christian family becomes an agent of evangelization by being what it is: the smallest gathering of the friends and followers of Christ.

Elaborate evangelization programs may be developed on the international and national levels. The day may come when Catholic evangelization agencies with huge budgets produce sophisticated programs for broadcast over cable television channels. Someday such television productions may bounce from one orbiting satellite to another twenty-four hours a day. Such agencies may produce movies for circulation to theaters all over the world.

But helpful as all this may turn out to be, nothing will ever match the importance and effectiveness of ordinary Christian families as they do their best to be small cells of Christian life. All the talk and all the "Christian entertainment" in the world can never match the potential impact of families who act on their convictions, who really strive to live their faith.

It remains true that "actions speak louder than words." As Paul VI said,

> The first means of evangelization is the witness of an authentically Christian life, given over to God in a communion that nothing should destroy and at the same time given to one's neighbor with limitless zeal.

The Christian family embodies a paradigmatic response to the command of Christ to love God and neighbor. Thus, the spirit and the lifestyle of the family call others by means of its simple witness to find life's meaning through a similar dedication to love of God and other people.

The purpose of evangelization, according to Paul VI, is first to invite others to conversion of heart. The family-church does this most effectively by the witness of its daily life. For the ideal toward which the Christian family strives is to order its entire existence according to this central thrust of the gospel. Though each family will do so "according to its lights" and according to its unique talents and character, the governing principle remains that of allowing the spirit of Christ to shine forth in all things. Again, Paul VI has written about this:

> Through this wordless witness these Christians stir up irresistible questions in the hearts of those who see how they live: Why are they like this? Why do they live in this way? What or who is it that inspires them? Why are they in our midst? Such a witness is already a silent proclamation of the Good News and a very powerful and effective one.

By placing the family first, by setting aside regular times to nourish marital and family relationships, the family-church proclaims the gospel. By serving one another and by a dedication to serving others with special needs, the family evangelizes. By its dedication to ordinary family prayer and ritual the family gives witness to the presence of Christ in its midst. By commitment to a local parish community the family proclaims that social and spiritual unity with others is vital to a Christian life. And by its efforts to be guided by the spirit of Christ rather than by the spirit of a merely secular culture, the family indicates to others that only through the love of God and neighbor do the pieces of the puzzle that is human existence take on a semblance of order.

But Paul VI points out that evangelization, if it is to be complete, will also take the form of words: "The Good News proclaimed by the witness of life sooner or later has to be proclaimed by the word of life."

What does this mean for a Christian family? That families ought to find ways to corner others and talk to them about the gospel? That families should go knocking on strangers' doors in an attempt to gain entry to their homes and talk about Christ? On the contrary, the last thing this means is that families should look for ways to "get pushy for Jesus." This approach is customary with certain fundamentalist sects, but it is alien to the perspectives of Catholicism, as well as alien to the spirit of virtually all of the mainline Protestant churches.

Again, Paul VI provides wise guidance: "The church is an evangelizer, but she begins by evangelizing herself." The family-church evangelizes itself first. This is one reason for the importance of all that has been discussed in this book so far. As a family, we act on our beliefs because we want our faith to shape our whole life, not just our words and our Sunday mornings. In the process, we say to ourselves over and over that we are disciples of Christ. In a very real sense, we proclaim the gospel to ourselves as we attempt to respond to the promptings of the Spirit.

There is another dimension of this self-evangelization. By our efforts to live the gospel, we reinforce in our own mind and heart an identity we have adopted, one which makes us different from many others. The Christian family views life and the world in ways that differ, sometimes considerably, from the perspectives of a secular culture. So we encourage one another and "build one another up" by means of the self-evangelization aspects of our Christian family lifestyle and spirituality.

Parents find themselves with a special role in the evangelization that goes on within the family. For parents remain at all times during their children's growing-up years their most influential and effective catechists. Parents have heard for a good number of years now that they are the primary religious educators of their children. But many still struggle with the everyday implications of this truth.

The kinds of catechesis that happen within the family are not only the most important from the perspective of the child's need for ongoing formation in the Christian life. Catechesis includes evangelization. That is, catechesis is a way to share with the child the basic message of the gospel.

This is where it becomes important for parents to feel comfortable with verbalizing their faith. Some Catholic parents may find it necessary to overcome a reluctance to talk about their life experience from a faith perspective. They may inherit this reticence from their own family of origin. Parental actions remain more important than words, but actions without verbal commentary will not have as great an impact on the child as a combination of the two.

Again Paul VI writes about this: "In the long run, is there any other way of handing on the gospel than by transmitting to another person one's personal experience of faith?" This is one challenge which confronts many Catholic parents today. Yet this verbalizing of parental faith is not to be understood so much as a matter of formal discussions about religion. This may happen now and then, but what matters most is that the parent be able to include the religious dimension of existence in his or her conversations with the child from the earliest days of life through to adulthood.

The two-year-old is fascinated with an insect as it crawls up the side of a tree. The "on-the-ball" parent may include in his or her sharing of the child's excitement a comment about how wonderful our good God must be to be able to make such a big tree and such a tiny bug.

Upon hearing about the divorce of a schoolmate's parents, the ten-year-old is anxious about his or her own parents' marriage. This is an opportunity for "God talk," a natural time to acknowledge the sacred and invoke God in genuine, nonpietistic ways, ways that simply include the sphere of the sacred in the conversation.

The teenager asks serious religious questions. The wise parent may simply join the budding adult in asking the same questions, in admitting the same doubts. This is a time to simply reassure the teenager that we are with him or her on the sometimes confusing paths of his or her search. Ready-made answers may hurt more than they help.

The parent who would be an effective evangelizer of his or her offspring is the one who resists the temptation to act as if responsibility for this aspect of parenting can be turned over to a Catholic school or a parish religious-education program. Seductive though this temptation may be, the realistic parent knows that it is a fool's dream, that it cannot be done, that the greatest impact on the child's religious development will happen, for good or for ill, within the context of family relationships.

Such parents expect no more than supplemental help from Catholic schools and parish religious education programs. They do what they can to understand faith on an adult level and to gain the fundamental knowledge and skills needed to incorporate faith and a Christian perspective into the normal events of family life.

Yet evangelization and catechesis within the family is by no means a one-way street. Paul VI says:

> The parents not only communicate the gospel to their children, but from their children they can themselves receive the same gospel as deeply lived by them.

Even the youngest child can provide parents with new insights into the Divine Mystery or the meaning of the gospel. By reflecting on their own best moments with their children, parents learn more about how God "feels" and "acts" in relationship to them. When parents stand back and let the toddler learn to walk by falling and getting up to try again, they learn that this is how God is with them too. Often the best parental behavior beautifully reflects the nature of God's relationship to the parent.

Even the most ordinary behavior of a child can teach parents more about the meaning of Jesus' words that we must become like a child if we would enter the Kingdom of Heaven. Words of Martin Luther illustrate some words from the Sermon on the Mount:

> Do as your children do. They go to bed at night and sleep without worries. They don't care whence they will get soup or bread tomorrow; they know that Father and Mother will take care of it.

Children evangelize their parents very well if the parents are open to this. They can gain many insights into the meaning of the old adage: "Act as if you had faith and faith will be given to you."

Yet the need to add words to evangelizing actions also finds expression outside the immediate family, in the community at large. Families that strive to allow the gospel to shape their life from the ground up tend to find themselves in situations where they can give public witness to their faith. One family was invited to participate in a city-wide forum on family life in the modern world. In the course of their participation, they were able to speak of the fundamental place of Christian faith in their family relationships and of its impact on their priorities and values.

Another family took part in a parish-organized outreach effort designed to extend an open invitation to "unchurched" members of their neighborhood to consider Catholicism. They did, in fact, knock on doors, introduce themselves and give to people an attractively printed leaflet on Catholicism and their parish community. Far from an attempt to "get pushy for Jesus," this evangelization effort was fashioned to extend a warm invitation to other families to consider the

Catholic way of life, if they did not already belong to a church community.

Evangelization does not mean the effort to proselytize or twist the arms of those who, with hardened hearts, resist the grace of God. Instead, it means trying to live what we say we believe: that love of God and other people is what life is all about.

In a secondary sense, evangelization means following up with words when the opportunity arises, both within the family and in situations outside the family circle. Evangelization means making a statement that the God who is love dwells among us, that this God can be trusted absolutely to care for us, and that therefore we are to turn our hearts away from, for example, the idols of the marketplace, in order to care for and love one another.

The Christian family-church is in a prime position to proclaim precisely this gospel in the modern world.

THE FAMILY SPIRIT:
IN BUT NOT OF THE WORLD

Chapter Ten

*I*n *St. Thomas Aquinas: The Dumb Ox*, a book written in the 1920s, G. K. Chesterton compared the condition of the Christian in the world to that of a huge old oak tree—roots deep in the earth, yet its topmost branches seem to almost touch the stars at night. This is also true of the Christian family. As an authentic form of *ekklesia*, the family is sent by Christ into the world to be for the world, to serve and love and care for God's creation and God's people. But at the same time, in words from the Letter to the Hebrews, the members of the home church are "strangers and foreigners on the earth . . . seeking a homeland" (Hebrews 11:13–14).

The condition of the Christian family is reflected in the words of Jesus in the Gospel of John:

> And now I am no longer in the world, but they are in the world . . . I have given them your word, and the world has hated them because they do not belong to the world, just as I do not belong to the world. I am not asking you to

take them out of the world, but I ask you to protect them from the evil one. They do not belong to the world, just as I do not belong to the world . . . As you have sent me into the world, so I have sent them into the world.

John 17:11–18

Traditionally, we summarize this strain of thought from the Fourth Gospel with the phrase "in but not of the world." It is imperative that both the "in" and the "not of" receive equal emphasis.

The so-called *Letter to Diognetus*, written in the late second or early third century, offers another, more detailed description of the Christian condition in the world:

For Christians cannot be distinguished from the rest of the human race by country or language or customs. They do not live in cities of their own; they do not use a peculiar form of speech; they do not follow an eccentric manner of life . . . They live in Greek and barbarian cities alike . . . and follow the customs of the country in clothing and food and other matters of daily living . . . They live in their own countries, but only as aliens . . . Every foreign land is their fatherland, and yet for them every fatherland is a foreign land . . . It is true that they are "in the flesh," but they do not live "according to the flesh." They busy themselves on earth, but their citizenship is in heaven . . . To put it simply: What the soul is in the body, that Christians are in the world. The soul is dispersed through all the members of the body, and Christians are scattered through all the cities of the world. The soul dwells in the body, but does not belong to the body, and Christians dwell in the world, but do not belong to the world.

In this excerpt from the *Letter to Diognetus*, we must make allowances for a body/soul dualism which seems out of place today. All the same, these words illustrate that the condition of the Christian family is "in but not of the world."

Another more contemporary way to express this same idea would be to say that the Christian family lives in a countercultural fashion. That is, the family strives to live according to standards and values sometimes at odds with those embraced by the dominant culture. On the other hand, it is also true that there is much about secular society in which the Christian family rejoices. So the family-church is not in favor of a gloom-and-doom outlook on life simply because it chooses to fashion its life in ways that conflict with some of the dominant trends in society at large. The Christian family is not convinced that the world is going to hell in a handbasket.

Nevertheless, what may be most evident about the spirituality of the Christian family and the lifestyle which arises from this spirituality are the ways in which the Christian family may choose to be different. Much about the life of the family-church may be countercultural, not in negative ways but in ways that make positive statements. In fact, much about a family spirituality in these pages reflects a countercultural stance rooted in the spirit of the gospel.

We said that the Christian family places a heavy emphasis on giving regular time to nourish family relationships and encourages its members to spend time in prayerful solitude. This is clearly a countercultural perspective in a society that values individualism on the surface, but insists on social conformity when the chips are down. It is also true that our society values "privacy," but not prayerful solitude.

The Christian family is serious—not to say grim—about a family dedication to serving others with special needs. This service orientation is countercultural in a society which believes in "looking out for Number One" and passing the buck to huge agencies and institutions when it comes to the poor, the underprivileged, the handicapped, and those dying of loneliness. There is nothing trendy about a dedication to serving others.

The Christian family, we said, develops ways for prayer and ritual to have a comfortable part in the normal ebb and flow of the family's daily life. This is countercultural in a world which would secularize family life along with every other aspect of society. Have any of us ever seen a television sitcom family or soap-opera family portrayed sharing mealtime prayer, outside of programs where this prayer is merely nostalgic or sentimental? Family prayer and ritual are countercultural in the extreme, for they reflect and nourish the family's relationship with the One who is the source and goal of the family's existence.

The foundation of the foundational church, in its traditional nuclear form, is the continuing promise of spouses to remain faithful to each other in love. So they make the sacrifices necessary to spend time with each another, apart from their children, regularly. This is crazy behavior in a society which views marriage as primarily a legal arrangement, lifelong marriage as a pipe dream, and divorce as the logical outcome of marriage. Thus, the spirituality of the married couple is countercultural, too.

We outlined the relationship between the family and the parish and pointed out how important these two forms of church are to each other. This, too, is countercultural. We live in a society which encourages families to live isolated from one another. In many cities, the traditional neighborhood and the traditional neighborhood parish are things of the past. To believe in the formation of family communities is to adhere to principles which are countercultural.

We also noted that spending time with children is more important than spending money on children. This principle may become more difficult to live out in our culture the older children become. All the same, it's important to keep the ideal alive. To highlight this attitude as part of Christian parenting is to encourage lack of support for our economic system, the ultimate principle of which is to buy as much as possible as often as possible whether we need it or not. Mass-media advertising pressures parents and kids to believe that giving children things is what the good parent does. To value committed personal relationships over the stockpiling of possessions is highly countercultural.

Two-parent and single-parent families are challenged by and find comfort in the same gospel with which all are presented. To respond to this gospel in authentically Christian ways will sometimes place the parents at odds with the values and attitudes of the dominant culture.

Without a fellow parent to offer support, the single parent may find it very difficult to resist pressures to buy, buy, buy, and go into debt to do it. On the other hand, if couple parents disagree about this or about how to interpret the ideal, that can be difficult, too. All the same, the ideal stands and is worth believing in.

We discussed ways in which a Christian view of human sexuality has an impact on a family spirituality and on the ways in which husband and wife may understand themselves and their roles. We live in a society which trivializes human sexuality and human relationships. The dominant culture encourages the alienation of men and women from their sexuality, as if sexuality were nothing but a way to have fun or feel good. A Christian approach to this dimension of human nature and human existence will often require the Christian family to think and believe in ways which a secularized world scorns.

Finally, when we discussed the ways the family proclaims the gospel, we emphasized the need for the family to allow the gospel to condition all aspects of its life. Truly, this is the most basic countercultural act. For to live like this is to place the true God above all the phony gods of a secularized culture—including the gods of materialism, violence, profit, and production—while at the same time embracing the good wherever it may be discovered.

To do this is to reject the popular conception of religion as "a private matter" with nothing significant to do with social or political issues. Consider, for example, the outrage from some sectors when the Catholic bishops of the United States were so bold as to address in the public forum the issue of the nuclear arms race. The dominant culture views religion as a private hobby, a ho-hum activity best isolated to Sunday mornings before professional sports organizations demand our presence in front of the television screen. Any attempt on the part of religion to violate these boundaries is labeled "religious fanaticism."

It is clear, then, that we have already presented in some detail the countercultural character of a Christian family spirituality. Yet there are other consequences of this "in but not of the world" condition that remain to be examined.

The role of television in the life of the family-church community requires constant vigilance. Many families today are concerned about the impact of television on the quality of family life. Families often find that much of the time they have together they hand over to watching television. But even if we watch several programs together as a family, our togetherness is superficial. Suggestions from educators that families watch a program together then turn off the set and discuss what they have watched seem naive. How many families find they have the power to turn off the set once it is on? Research even suggests that television can become an addictive "drug," so that it no longer matters what is being watched; all that matters is watching. Numerous studies, as well as the experience of many ordinary families, indicate that heavy television watching has destructive effects on parent/child relationships.

One of the facts about commercial television which the Christian family may take most seriously has to do with the role of television in the moral formation of the person. As early as 1975, the Administrative Board of the U. S. Catholic Conference published a document on television and family life. In this document, we find the following statement: "In our society today, television is the single most formative influence in shaping people's attitudes and values."

Words to give the Christian parent pause.

The values and attitudes proclaimed by commercial television may be summarized in one statement: "The good life depends on the unlimited acquisition of money and possessions." What we own is more important than what we are. Appearances matter more than reality. We should be willing to do anything we can get away with to become as affluent as possible. In other words, that business about the camel and the eye of a needle is a lot of foolishness. (See Mark 10:25.)

There are families who decide that life is more sane and human with no television at all. Our family has been without television since 1976, before our first child was born. Our three sons have grown up in a television-free environment, and none of us seems to have suffered any debilities from the experience. In 1994, we bought a video viewer which looks like a small television set but can be used only to play video cassettes. This was the extent of our compromise, even in the face of occasional objections from our offspring.

Other families limit television watching to one hour a day, with exceptions now and then for special programs. After the initial "withdrawal" period, the children in such families invariably decide that life with little or no television is quite a good life.

Christian family members may find themselves asking in all seriousness if there are not better ways to be well informed and to find entertainment than watching television—reading newspapers, books, and magazines, for example, and playing games or going for walks. They may decide that there are forms of entertainment which are far more beneficial, on both the personal and family levels. A family can gain far more from a leisurely walk around the block together than from thirty minutes of group television watching.

A Christian family spirituality is also sensitive to issues of social justice and peace and to ways in which the family can have a positive impact on society at large. The family may become aware of the injustices which continue to exist due to racism. They may or may not join picket lines, but they can make efforts to sensitize both children and parents to the equality of all races and to the consequences of both personal and institutional forms of racism.

Art and decorations in the home can be used to reflect various races and their cultures. Children, especially when they are very young, can be exposed to music from other cultures by means of recordings from a public library. It is a simple matter, also, to subscribe to a magazine or two which feature photographs of various racial groups. Parents can be sensitive to racial stereotypes in children's books and be prepared to counter these.

Of course, many families are fortunate enough to live in cities where several races mix to make up the population. In such places, there are many opportunities to learn an appreciation for racially and ethnically distinct values, if the family decides to involve itself at the right times in the right places.

Sexism is another justice issue which the family may strive to counteract. By distributing household chores with no regard for what is traditionally "men's work" and "women's work," the Christian family can form children and adults who are better prepared to oppose sexism in both society and the church. If children see that Mom and Dad treat one another as equals—that Mom takes out the garbage about as often as Dad and Dad cleans house, washes dishes, and does the laundry; if they see that Mom can change the oil in the car and has an important role to play in "bringing home the bacon" they will be less likely to be affected by sexism than many of their peers.

In the Christian family, there should be no support for placing women "on a pedestal" in order to keep them "in their place." There may be some stimulating discussions around the family table as girls discover that women may not become priests.

War and peace is another issue which may have significant impact on a Christian family's spirituality. Many families accept with enthusiasm the U. S. bishops' invitation to fast from meat on Fridays as a way to pray for peace. This is but one way in which families can allow issues of war and peace to touch their life. Parents may find themselves called upon to support teenage sons as they struggle with their feelings about draft registration.

Closely related to issues of war and peace is the Christian thrust toward nonviolence in human relationships. By learning and making use of techniques for the nonviolent resolution of family conflicts, a Christian family may be better prepared to adopt a Christian position on the place of nonviolence in national and international disputes.

Underlying the Christian family's interest and involvement in issues such as those mentioned here is the conviction that citizenship is subordinate to faith, that the Christian is called to embrace the gospel before he or she is called to salute the flag. The Christian family understands perfectly well the famous words of St. Thomas More just before he was beheaded: "The king's good servant, but God's first."

The fact that it is a family which is involved in these issues is of special significance. We must never underestimate the symbolic value of family involvement in peace and justice issues. Although the idea receives more lip service than serious attention, it remains true that the family is the most basic building block of society. When families begin to change their lifestyle and become active on social issues, elected leaders pay attention. They are well aware that the next thing they feel may be the shaking of the foundations.

Another way the Christian family may become countercultural is in the cultivation of quiet in the home. We live in a world made noisy by technology: cars; motorcycles; jackhammers; television sets and radios; computer games that crash, roar and beep; air conditioners that hum and hum; appliances that wash and dry; gadgets that whir, buzz, roar, clatter, and ping.

It seems nearly impossible to manufacture a child's mechanical toy without including a noisemaker of some kind. Children learn from an early age that in order to have a good time they must make noise.

It is nearly normal for the American home to never be quiet, unless everyone is asleep, and sometimes not even then. How many people fall asleep each night in front of a still-glowing and flickering television set? We feel compelled to turn on a radio to drive away the quiet in our homes and in our cars. Many people leave a television set on whether they are watching it or not. Some parents take it for granted that teenagers are constitutionally incapable of doing homework without the music of their subculture playing loudly in the same room.

Everywhere we go there is background music, even in elevators and even when some store or business puts us on hold on the telephone.

Some families choose to take back some control over this dimension of their life, to build in quiet times in the family environment. A few simple rules can make an enormous difference. One family decided that, as a general rule, when there are two or more people in the family car at the same time, the radio will not be turned on. They now find that more talking happens on both short and long trips in the car

This same family decided to accept the rule that no music is allowed while doing homework. Not so remarkably, a positive effect has been noticed on the quality of schoolwork being done and on the grades being brought home.

Another family set 9:00 p.m. as the hour when, on weekdays, all noise makers must be turned off. No television, no music, no blender in the kitchen going whir-grind-whir. At a family meeting, all agreed that this was a good decision. Each family member could tell of ways in which the quiet has been good for him or her.

Another family, which belongs to a religious tradition known to be outside the mainstream, simply owns none of the domestic conveniences like television sets, radios, and power lawn mowers. Their home strikes the visitor like an island of quiet in an ocean of noise. Though this family's beliefs about cultivating quiet may strike most as extreme, there is no arguing with the obvious fact that the children in this home are more calm, more quiet, than the typical ten- and twelve-year-old.

The various traditional spiritualities which developed over the centuries all agree on this point—that quiet and stillness are necessary to the spiritual, physical, and emotional health of the person. It is of value, if nothing else, to be able to hear oneself think now and then.

A Christian family may feel a need to take some steps toward making life a bit more quiet, especially in the family environment of the home. To do so, of course, is countercultural in a world which swims in noise as a fish swims in water. At the same time, however, this may be one of the more manageable ways in which the Christian family can allow its lifestyle to be shaped by an "in but not of the world" spirituality. All it takes is the decision to do it.

When families decide to take charge of their life, to regain some of the control over their life which was unwittingly and gradually turned over to influences outside the family circle; when families begin to reclaim the power to shape their own values and pass along to children a living religious tradition in place of the gods of the dominant culture, society can't help but be affected.

Families have the power to change the world. One important aspect of a family spirituality is the challenge presented to families to take one giant step forward, and to do just that.

Afterword

*O*ne of the major themes of the Gospel of Matthew appears in these words of Matthew's Jesus: "None of those who cry out 'Lord, Lord,' will enter the kingdom of God but only the one who does the will of my Father in heaven" (Mt. 7:21).

There is a constant temptation, in our time as in all times, to act as if religion has little to do with reality. Thus we observe the common inclination to live as if baptism and the profession of a religious creed need have only peripheral impact on our life as a family. There is the tendency to limit faith to words, to allow faith to dictate actions mainly on Sunday mornings and at times when the consequences of doing so will have little effect on the fabric of our life "in the real world" and in our home.

A family spirituality first conditions the "being" of the family; it is more about what the family *is* than about what the family *does*. A family spirituality involves a simple, lived dedication to Christ in the real world. It is about prayer, faith, serving others, and so forth, of course. But because it is about such, it is also about laughter, about being foolish in the eyes of "the world," and about a great affection for a good party.

The spirituality for families suggested in these pages inspires us to say yes at times, no at others. It means we embrace the world with love and compassion, but we also call a spade a spade. Because of our family spirituality, we share life and faith together in ways which are always changing as both offspring and parents grow older, as the calendar pages fall and we need new ways to be a family.

It's easy to see the holiness in our family in retrospect, when we take out the old photographs or the old videos and remember "the good old days." One goal of a family spirituality is to help us see the goodness and holiness in our family here and now. The spirituality we share also prompts us to nourish one another as individuals, to encourage individual action and growth.

A family spirituality is one that is in-process, undergoing transformation even as it transforms us and the life we share. As a family, we are not the same now as we were last year or last month, and neither is our spirituality, our continuing efforts to follow the lead of Gospels in ways that make sense for our time and our place.

It must also be said, however, that the topic of family spirituality is, in large measure, unexplored territory. Families of all kinds are scouting out the terrain, learning from both their successful and unsuccessful efforts. In this, the kind of parish community to which they belong either helps or handicaps them. An awesome responsibility rests with parish leaders today to support families in order to nourish the roots of the church.

An authentic Christian spirituality for families makes of the family what tradition teaches it is meant to be "the first form of the church on earth" (Leo XIII) and a school of the Christian life. This family kind of spirituality brings us home, to one another and to God.

Suggestions for Further Reading

Barbeau, Clayton C. *Delivering the Male: Out of the Tough-Guy Trap into a Better Marriage* (Ikon Press, 1984). How to overcome the straitjacket aspects of the traditional male role in marriage. A great "examination of conscience" book for men, married or not.

—*The Father of the Family: A Christian Perspective*, revised and updated by Mitch Finley (Ikon Press, 1990). A modern classic; an inspiring and informative reflection on the various aspects of the Christian father's identity and vocation. Excellent.

Cline, Foster W., M. D., and Jim Ray. *Parenting Teens with Love & Logic: Preparing Adolescents for Responsible Adulthood* (Piñon Press, 1992). Applies the love-and-logic approach to parenting teenagers. "Required reading" for parents of teens.

—*Parenting with Love & Logic: Teaching Children Responsibility* (Piñon Press, 1990). How to implement a love-and-logic approach to parenting with younger children. Parents win because they learn to establish effective control without resorting to anger, threats, and power struggles. Kids win because they get to learn responsibility by solving their own problems at an early age. You can't do better than this book.

Curran, Dolores. *Family Prayer* (St. Anthony Messenger Press, 1983). An outstanding update of an earlier book. One of the most realistic and practical books on the topic.

—*Traits of a Healthy Family: Fifteen Traits Commonly Found in Healthy Families by Those Who Work with Them* (HarperSanFrancisco, 1985). "Must" reading for parents; excellent on virtually every aspect of practical family living. Ideal "spiritual reading" for anyone with family interests.

DeGidio, Sandra. *Enriching Faith Through Family Celebrations* (Twenty-Third Publications, 1989). An excellent collection of rituals for families for every season of the year, prefaced by an outstanding short essay on what family prayer and rituals are all about.

Finley, Kathleen. *Dear God: Prayers for Families with Children* (Twenty-Third Publications, 1995). A collection of short, delightfully illustrated prayers for just about any everyday or special family occasion.

Finley, Mitch. *Your Family in Focus: Appreciating What You Have, Making It Even Better* (Ave Maria Press, 1993). A discussion of all aspects of family life with the emphasis on helping parents and couples feel better about the family project they are about.

Gudorf, Christine E. *Body, Sex & Pleasure: Reconstructing Christian Sexual Ethics* (Pilgrim Press, 1994). An academic work, but filled with mind-expanding suggestions on ways we can cultivate appreciation, not rejection and shame, of our bodies and our sexuality.

Hays, Edward. *Prayers for the Domestic Church: A Handbook for Worship in the Home* (Forest of Peace Publishing, 1989). A fine collection of longer prayers and rituals for virtually every occasion, with informative introductory sections.

Kavanaugh, John Francis S. J. *Following Christ in a Consumer Society: The Spirituality of Cultural Resistance* (Orbis, 1991). Examines the impact of faith on everyday lifestyle issues. An excellent, inspiring book.

Luebering, Carol. *Your Child's First Communion: A Look at Your Dreams* (St. Anthony Messenger Press, 1984). Perhaps the best resource on preparing a child for First Communion, this pamphlet is easy to read and filled with delightful suggestions and insights.

McDonald, Patrick J. and Claudette M. McDonald. *The Soul of a Marriage* (Paulist Press, 1995). Helpful reflections on a spirituality of marriage that can help couples see God at work in their day-to-day lives with each other.

McGinnis, Kathleen, and James McGinnis. *Parenting for Peace & Justice: Ten Years Later* (Orbis Books, 1990). Excellent book; loaded with ideas rooted in family experience.

Nelson, Gertrud Mueller. *To Dance with God: Family Ritual and Community Celebration* (Paulist Press, 1986). The author discusses the history, psychology, and spirituality of ritual in general and Christian ritual in particular, drawing frequently on her own experience of family life.

Roberto, John, ed. *Family Rituals and Celebrations*, (Don Bosco Multimedia, 1992). This book is designed to help us enrich our family's faith life and sense of togetherness in simple, practical ways. A great way to gain a better understanding of family prayer and rituals and how to do them. One volume in the very helpful "Catholic Families Series."

Roberts, Challon O'Hearn and William P. Roberts. *Partners in Intimacy: Living Christian Marriage Today* (Paulist Press, 1988). Excellent reading. Provides many practical insights into the various facets of Christian marriage.

Stinnett, Nick and John DeFrain. *Secrets of Strong Families* (Berkley Books, 1986). What makes a family healthy and resilient? The authors present the answer here, and it is not that a family must be conflict-free. Great reading. Also available from Cokesbury (Nashville, TN) in a videocassette (30 minutes, in color, 1988).

Travnikar, Rock, O. F. M. *The Blessing Cup: Forth Simple Rites for Family Prayer-Celebrations* (St. Anthony Messenger Press, 1994). An excellent practical resource for families of all kinds.

Winn, Marie. *The Plug-in Drug: Television, Children & the Family* (Viking Penguin, 1985). Challenges popular attitudes concerning the impact of television on child development and the quality of family relationships. "Required reading" for parents.

Wright Wendy M. *Sacred Dwelling: A Spirituality of Family Life* (Forest of Peace Publishing, 1994). A wonderful collection of reflections on the meaning of family life and the sacred times that are unique to it.